# Fish On!

Techniques, Tips, and True Life
Experiences from a 25-Year Trout
and Smallmouth Guide on the
Connecticut River

*John Marshall*

❖❖❖❖❖❖❖❖

By
John Marshall

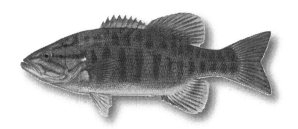

# Fish On!

LCCN 2009912661

ISBN 1449906516

9 8 7 6 5 4 3 2 1

# Table of Contents:

*Continued...*

************

# Dedication

This book is dedicated to my wife, Susan. Her patience, support and understanding through 38 years of marriage and 25 years guiding enabled my achieving continued success in a challenging career.

I honor the memory of Wally Kolkowski – my friend and fly fishing mentor over 37 years ago. I met Wally as a young man in my mid twenties with a strong desire to learn fly fishing and he an accomplished married fly fisherman without children in his mid sixties. I was hungry for fly fishing knowledge and Wally needed someone to share it with. It was a perfect match. Everything he knew about fly fishing was shared (including his favorite places) while I absorbed valuable information like a sponge. Wally also gave me carte blanche to his specialized and extensive private fishing library. Wally Kolkowski provided the direction and tools while clearing a path for me to follow through while on my fly fishing journey. I am and will always be grateful.

I thank Fred Arbona, Al Caucci and Bob Nastasi, Ed Engle, Kenn Filkins, Art Flick, Charles Fox, Rick Hafele, Renne Harrop, Ed Koch, Gary LaFontaine, Vincent Marinaro, Bill McMillan, Charles Meck, Sylvester Nemes, Carl Richards and Doug Swisher, Ernest Schweibert, John Shewey, Neale Streeks, and Dave Whitlock for

1

their books and articles. By integrating their great work, Wally's gift to me, and the information gained from thousands of hours on stream, I was able to advance towards a better understanding and appreciation for my chosen species.

This dedication would not be complete without thanking Dave Cleveland of Woodstock, Vermont. Throughout the years, when not guiding, I enjoyed fishing with numerous fishing companions. Most had the ulterior motive of taking their fly fishing to another level. I was more than happy to oblige as my goal is and always has been to help others to enhance their enjoyment of the outdoors – especially when fishing. Dave used a different approach. He wanted nothing for himself except to enjoy the company of another fellow angler. His encouragement, friendship, generosity and honesty has provided a refreshing encounter and is over-whelmingly appreciated.

John Marshall

# INTRODUCTION:

Few American Rivers are more beautifully framed than the Connecticut as she flows from her headwaters between New Hampshire and Vermont and through to the Connecticut River Valley below Sumner Falls.

There are lush bordering farmlands, rolling hills and picturesque mountains. Giant coniferous trees align the higher elevations, while near the river a mix leaning towards deciduous. They offer shade and protection from erosion.

It's a beautiful frame and a living one. The cast of wildlife is numerous and includes bear, beaver, deer, fox, mink, moose, muskrat, otter, turtles and weasel. Birders have a good chance to view ducks, eagles, geese, great blue herons, green herons, kingfishers, osprey, red tail hawks, sand pipers, snowy white egrets and shore and songbirds. Mid May through October presents us with an excellent late spring thru early fall fishery of feisty Smallmouth Bass taking advantage of the incredibly rich forage base of insects, crustaceans, bait fish and terrestrials.

This beautiful river bares her soul by presenting historians a wealth of information.

From the hard fought battles and disputes throughout the centuries, the legendary log drives which claimed lives every year to the rejuvenation of America's most scenic sewer, the Connecticut River now stands tall and proud as one of the countries 14 great heritage rivers.

As maturity absorbs our frivolous youth we begin to realize that our greatest wealth, our most precious treasures lie within us in memories. These are the only things we truly own. Everything else comes and goes. The Connecticut River between New Hampshire and Vermont is beyond compare in sharing so many quality, outdoor memorable moments while inspiring people from all over the world.

My name is John Marshall and this is how I feel about my home river.

I started 25 years ago as a predominant Licensed & Registered Fishing Guide for trout offering McKenzie Drift

Boat Float Trips on the hallowed water of the Upper Connecticut River in northern New Hampshire. (This enabled adding a chapter with valuable insights towards pursuing trout). My guests fished one of four different sections equaling 30 miles of prime trout water beginning in West Stewartstown, New Hampshire and ending in South Stratford, New Hampshire.

It is a lovely piece of river containing long pools and flats with the occasional transition from riffle to rapid to run bordered by shade producing tree lined banks, forested rolling hills and mountains.

During summertime low water conditions the water temperature is too warm for consistent trout fishing beyond early morning or evening hours. Stressing the fish at this time would most surely limit their ability to survive when released. It was during this period you could find me guiding for smallmouth bass 125 miles to the south on the same river. They thrive during these conditions. By mid September guiding for brook, brown and rainbow trout resumes.

Five years ago my guiding operations began to focus more toward smallmouth bass which are closer to home. The growing interest in this species along with the beautiful places they are found prompted the move plus I flat out enjoy fishing for them. I now only offer the occasional trout float on the upper river when not guiding for bass. This decision should have been made years earlier but pride in my ability to help guests deceive the challenging trout of the Upper C kept us working that water.

Perhaps there is a river or piece of water which has an effect on you. If smallmouth bass live in its waters and you are interested in pursuing them as an angler this writing will provide helpful information towards finding, hooking, playing and landing them. While geared towards float fishing for river bass, the wading or shore angler will find information here useful as will those who frequent ponds and smaller lakes. Fly fishing is emphasized with a chapter dedicated to help you improve fly fishing skills, however spinning is well represented. Many of the tactics discussed can be used successfully for smallmouth and trout while fly fishing or spinning.

You will not find every piece of information about smallmouth bass here or all the flies, lures, plugs and soft plastics which are available to catch them. I have listed those offerings which have afforded a good deal of success at different times. This project is an accumulation of many years of on the river float experience. The information within is presented in a way which will enable the reader an immediate degree of success depending on the time and effort applied and the water fished. It is meant to enable a person with little or no experience using a small boat on moving water to safely and successfully hook up with smallmouth bass using a straight forward "Keep it Simple," approach.

I also included a chapter describing a days guiding with insights and thoughts as they occur to, from and during the days fishing with guests. This may be quite helpful for those considering a guiding career. Following this chapter are a few stories from my own personal fishing experiences which took place in rivers and streams of Upstate New York while pursuing large rainbow trout (steelhead). I hope you find them enjoyable and entertaining.

John Marshall
July 2009, Hartland Four Corners, Vermont

************

# Understanding Our Quarry:

The successful pursuit of these river bass requires learning how they adapt feeding patterns and movement to the ever changing challenges of the section of river chosen and the present weather or river conditions.

There will be days when the smallmouth or any other fish are just not willing. This could be caused by poor river conditions such as heavily stained water or an approaching front, a brisk wind, decrease or increase in temperature, dam releases that are too large or too small, an on-going drought or numerous other variables. The bass may have started their annual journey back down river to the deeper wintering waters. These will all have an effect on where these fish hold and how active they feed.

Smallmouth live in an underwater environment causing them to react to river changes in a way which will afford them the best chance for survival. It has been my experience that the most difficult fishing for smallmouth will occur in heavily stained water with large dam releases or on windy days with an approaching front. Before, during or after a mild approaching weather system fishing can improve. A mild front offers more positive results than a more pronounced one. Very good fishing can be expected during light or intermittent showers with little or no wind. Overcast calm days are much more welcome than bright sunlight.

I can recall numerous floats with guests for trout during overcast days on the Upper Connecticut River. The fish were surface feeding on the huge pools and flats showing their positions and taking our flies with a complete lack of caution. My guests were pleased and life was easy. Whenever sunlight would break through the clouds those rising trout would shut down as quickly and completely as if someone turned on a light switch. Surface action stopped and the fish became weary and more difficult to approach and deceive. When clouds would again block out the influence of the sun the trout would begin rising. The same applies for bass. I learned that bright sunlight is not my friend when fishing. A brisk wind will also put off a surface bite for trout as well as smallmouth. There are exceptions but as a general rule this holds true for river smallmouth and trout.

Most of the seasonal smallmouth bass fishing on the

Connecticut River below Wilder Dam are for fish which winter in the deeper pools above Bellows Falls Dam. They begin their spring migration upriver in April to spawn with groups spreading out up to 30 miles.

They may travel just 100 yards from their wintering areas for the spring ritual or all the way up to 30 plus miles. This depends on genetics, size of the stream or river, incoming streams, available spawning habitat for numbers of fish and also if everything necessary for their survival such as gravel, depth, feed, structure, cover, rocky terrain and adjoining areas of depth is present. With the proper habitat, food base and protection from pollution, predators and over harvest, these entertaining battlers will propagate in a given section of river to full holding potential.

Early spawning begins when the water temperature reaches 57 to 58 degrees with most occurring in the 60 to 62 degree range. There will still be some bass spawning all the way to 70 degrees. Look for circular gravel and small rock depressions lighter in color than the surrounding area, from 1 to 2 feet in diameter. The males will prepare these nests a week or two before the spawning when water temperatures are in the mid to upper fifties. (This is the temperature bass begin to feed more actively all the way into the low eighties). The spawning females and accompanying males located will be aggressive and less susceptible to an anglers lack of stealth during this period. After spawning, the females will retreat to deeper quiet water for a week or two to recover, eating and moving little during this period.

Bass do not all spawn at once. There will be fish in pre spawn, spawn, post spawn resting and post spawn feeding stage from two to four weeks. They can all be deceived into striking however recent post spawn fish will be more challenging usually requiring a slow retrieve near the bottom. Those bass which move upriver will stay near the spawning grounds for the summer months taking advantage of the easy living providing good habitat, abundant crawfish, baitfish, stream born insects and terrestrials, etc. are available. From early September thru early October most gravitate back to the deeper pools downstream fattening up along the way in preparation for the winter months. The following spring after ice out it all begins again.

Less movement usually will take place if suitable habitat and feed is nearby. There will need to be ample food to sustain them during the fall and winter months. Smallmouth can still be caught with soft plastics, deep-diving plugs, lures, flies and bait until mid December and beyond. The river here usually freezes for ice fishing by then.

The ability of a person to identify and cast to the right places, choose and manipulate a lure, plug, soft plastic or fly properly at the correct depth, set the hook and maintain a steady tension throughout the battle will all contribute to the numbers of fish hooked and landed.

If you are a person who has experienced little fish catching action in the past read on. If you have ever received several strikes or more on an outing yet were only able to hook one or two read on. If some days produce several hookups but few fish landed definitely read on.

The goal here is for the suggestions and shared experience acquired from thousands of float trips to help you gain a better understanding while enabling you to find, hook and land several more fish when on future outings.

Remember, the fish are not there just waiting to jump on your flies or lures. Few floats will produce active fish from the beginning to end of the day. The feeding activity of smallmouth changes daily and often many times during the day. The feeding level for active fish can vary from hour to hour. Sometimes the bass will accept food on the surface, sometimes mid depth, sometimes near the bottom and on active days all three. On inactive days the key place is near the bottom.

Try to stay in tune with the feeding rhythms while making fly or lure changes along with depth, and retrieve adjustments. A change in size can also be a triggering factor, especially when missing strikes.

Different plugs and lures are designed to be fished at different depths. Some are versatile and can be fished at many depths depending on the retrieve, diameter of the line used or if it is rigged with or without weight. The same holds true for flies while using floating, sink tip and full sinking fly lines. Try to find the right offering at the correct depth with the action and speed of retrieval which brings strikes.

Begin a day by casting into the bank with a surface offering. If little or no action try the area which gains depth when moving away from the bank. This is the first drop off. If not successful, work your way down to the bottom looking for the area, depth and action the bass are willing to strike. A golfer will not use the same club for every hole. Be versatile while trying to discover which depth and type of water the bass are most receptive.

Certain areas have high percentage top water or just below the surface fishing potential. Sometimes a mid depth Rapala or Rapala type plug will offer a higher percentage opportunity or a deep diving crank bait may be the right animal. Soft plastic jerk baits (flukes), swim baits, tubes, jigs or plastic worms fished top to bottom may offer better results. Fly fishermen or women will also be able to find and enjoy top water (surface) opportunities, as well as subsurface. Floating a river several times will help in learning the best offerings, the correct depth etc., dependent upon the habitat, weather, river conditions and where follows or strikes occur. This can change day to day.

Someone who has not experienced the thrill of a ferocious, heart stopping surface strike may ask why all the fuss over a fish which has an average size on most rivers of one half to two pounds (depending on the size of the river, habitat and available food) and a top weight here of seven pounds? Aggressive strikes can make your heart jump when occurring visually on the surface. Their leaps are electric and many, they battle hard all the way to the net and are found in beautiful environments.

It was no easy task for these battlers to capture the respect and admiration of a dyed-in-the-wool trout fisherman beyond the source of guiding potential. In many ways, I feel like a past Boston Red Sox fan who now cheers for the New York Yankees. My clients over the years, have caught and released thousands of trout and smallmouth bass. A constant in almost every situation is a smallmouth could tow an equal size trout at will.

We would treasure that magic moment when immediately following a hookup we realized that a big trout was on the end of my guest's line. This knowledge is usually transmitted by a power surge throughout the connection with the uncontrolled taking of lots of line quickly or the trophy visibly reveals itself by jumping.

It is something special (when either fly fishing or spinning) to feel the electricity of a large wild trout as it breaks water time and time again knowing the connection most times is frail. It is heart stopping excitement.

Will this trophy shake loose or is the tippet strong enough? Don't give any slack, keep the right amount of tension, do not put too much pressure. Man, if we can only get a better look and please allow this gentleman to land this fish are a few more of the concerns and thoughts which consume one during this special encounter.

A fisherman may make hundreds of casts in pursuit of a large wild trout. (This is relative to the location but usually 19 inches or better is considered a nice fish). It is so satisfying to land one when fortunate enough to hook up and hauntingly disappointing to lose a large fish because opportunities come few and far between.

At first it is acceptable to catch numbers of smallmouth or trout but after gaining a little experience each hookup is anticipated as the sought-after trophy. A desire to deceive a larger specimen replaces quantity.

With more experience we are now in search of that trophy fish with a brief hope of encountering a big one at every hookup. When we see that a hookup is not trophy sized, the hooked fish is usually played, enjoyed, landed, and then carefully released. The next hookup offers the same hope for a big fish and then the same process. This is the transformation nearly every fisherman goes through.

Enter the smallmouth bass. Smallmouth in my home river are all wild. They usually strike much more viciously than a large wild trout, especially when feeding on or near the surface - not for the faint of heart. They jump higher, fight harder, battle longer and are equal or more intense in electricity. They are more aggressive and usually less selective. The best part is that every smallmouth hooked offers us this same characteristic no matter what its size.

The average size bass here is on to two-plus pounds with specimens every day going three to four and even a few honest five plus pound fish hooked and released during a season. There are still plenty of one quarter to half pound and one pound smallmouth available .
They frequent areas which afford them greater protection from being devoured such as large sunken trees or boulders, stones and rip rap containing many nooks and crannies. The presence of these smaller fish tell us that this is a stepladder fishery of the future having dif-

ferent classes of fish. If all these positives are placed together it is easy to understand why smallmouth bass have become so popular with both fly fishing and spinning anglers. They are a fun fish.

The prime area we fish for smallmouth bass on the Connecticut River is below Wilder Dam in Wilder, Vermont to Bellows Fall Dam in Bellow Falls, Vermont, from early May through mid October. This is 35+ miles of prime smallmouth water. The river portrays her diversity here by supporting many fishable species. There is a terrific insect population.

Abundant crustaceans (crawfish) and baitfish provide an excellent forage base as do terrestrial opportunities such as beetles, grasshoppers, ants, mice, frogs, baby birds, etc. The dominant food source will be crawfish, baitfish and insects including the larger Dobson flies (hellgrammites) and fish flies but these fish will frequently attack as diversified opportunists.

Pockets of northern pike relate to vegetation patches, blow downs and structure with drop offs and slower deeper water nearby. Walleye can be found around shoals and islands with moderate current and drop offs. Trout (good sized because of the rivers mass and the food it is able to support) are found below dams, in or adjacent to the fastest water, near springs, drop offs and where tributaries enter.

Then of course, there is the smallmouth bass - The star of the show. They frequent areas such as banks, cuts in the bank, set backs, rocks, boulders and ledge, downed trees, points, bank hugging rip rap extending to the first drop off, shoals and islands, seams, weed beds, bridge supports, docks, shaded areas and any change in depth. A depth change is easily noticeable by a transition from light to dark water along with a difference of visibility. The bottom is quite visible close to the area of darkness and limited visibility. This is where a depth change occurs.

The shoreline bank is a good place to start but sometimes the bass will not be holding or taking here. They may be holding on the first drop off from the bank. This is where a change of water depth occurs as you move from the bank toward the middle of the river. Anytime a change of depth exists, even a small change of a foot or two is a good place to cast, especially if there is some sort of structure in the area. Even shallow flats and shoreline mini pools and cuts with only a foot or two of depth will often produce.

The fish which prowl here are fish actively seeking food and can be quite aggressive if unaware of your presence. They will be spooky because of the lack of depth and their vulnerability to predators. Cast slightly beyond, to the side or up from the target and bring the lure, plug or fly seductively into the sweet spot.

Present your offering where there are small changes in an ecosystem offering these fish protection from the current and/or some sort of cover or structure. A quiet small pool like area near the bank surrounded by slightly faster water is a good target. A bank offering shade from trees with the addition of a blowdown, deeper water, rip rap, ledge, a current break, rocky bottom, large stone or even boulders are the type of targets we are looking to cast to. Cast above, below and to the edges where shallow riffles and slightly deeper rapids exhibit a change in depth. Another good target is where a rapid spills over a ledge.

Cover can be a high or undercut bank, an overhanging tree, lily pads, a large ledge or rock or it could be something man made such as a dock, bridge, boat, raft, etc., all providing protection from sunlight and a degree of safety from direct overhead attack from a predator. Structure can be a downed tree laying in the water, lily pads or grasses, any size rock from golf ball to truck sized or ledge or again even something man made such as pilings, bridge supports, etc. These objects provide a current break from where to rest or feed and also may give safety from predators. Several mini pond areas of quiet water can be created by structure. These offer fish catching opportunities.

They are all potential hot spots. It may be an indentation in a shoreline (mini set backs in the bank), a rocky bank extending into the water with a lack of river current and depth or a blow down creating numerous nooks and crannies to explore. Slow moving quiet sections of bank with blow downs, small rocks to large boulders and submerged vegetation, offer good possibilities. A dock, a moored boat, pilings & rip rap can also attract fish. It's all good.

Always look for targets to cast to. When two or more different shoreline cover or structure features come together make sure to get something in there especially in quiet water near the bank.

Each float is an adventure, refreshing for the mind and body. Every float is different. The river never remains exactly the same.

It is my goal to share experience and knowledge so that fishing enthusiasts may enjoy their river as I do and in the process realize there are other inspiring species to pursue other than trout. Sometimes smallmouth can be very easy to catch and then there are those days they will be extremely difficult. The pieces of the puzzle need to be put together to create opportunities on those inactive days.

I have had an unquenchable thirst for fishing knowledge throughout the past few decades with a focus towards smallmouth bass and trout in rivers and streams. This hopefully is reflected in the following pages. Your own fishing success will benefit from the experience and knowledge learned throughout the years and shared in this writing.

My desire is to help others enjoy an outdoor fishing experience in a way which would be difficult or impossible on their own. A pearl or two gained from reading a how-to book is time well spent. My hope is to offer several pearls.

We catch one fish at a time. It is impossible to land the second, third or fourth until you catch the first. Be alert, focused and perceptive. Try to make good decisions while staying observant on a slow day and turn it into a good day. Every time out something new can be learned. This applies to even the most experienced anglers.

Take the time to enjoy all the sights and sounds associated with a river float trip. Too many times my guests are so focused on the fishing aspect they forget to notice the beautiful scenery, the wild creatures all around them or hear the songbird orchestra of melodies always evident. Listen and you will hear them. Enjoy the entire experience. There is so much more than just the fishing.

************

# Fly Equipment for Smallmouth

## Fly Rods

An 8-1/2 to 9 foot rod for a 6 to 8 weight line is my preference. This is dependent upon the water to be fished and the size of the flies which will be used. It is much more pleasant to cast large size 2 to size 4 hair bugs, poppers and large sub surface offerings with a 7 or 8 weight rod. If the predominant flies used will be in the size 6 to 10 range or smaller a 6 or even 5 weight rod will give a more pleasurable experience.

Will you be fishing a large river or a small stream? Are the fish generally large trophy size or the smaller half pounders? A larger body of water may require a 7 or 8 weight rod where a 4, 5 or 6 weight rod will be the perfect animal for a smaller stream when casting smaller flies. River born smallmouth bass are very strong with excellent stamina, especially on larger rivers with current. Many folks do not wish to place that kind of wear and tear on a 4 or 5 weight rod. A lifetime of use can be inflicted from a fish or two on a lighter rod especially if a 4 pound smallmouth is able to power into the current. With the fish using the current to their advantage the resistance will then double or triple.

Bottom Line: Many casts will be required in the covering of the water during an outing. A rod which will enable this without excessively tiring the caster is important. A lower rated rod and line is lighter, easier to cast and more pleasurable when using dry fly imitations, poppers and smaller nymphs and streamers no larger than a size 6 - 10.

Some six weights are very light with a feel of a five. They cast size 6 - 12 flies in the 25 to 50 foot range by the average angler, consistently, precisely and with little effort. The seven or eight weight rod can cast large flies by the average angler in the 30 to 60 foot range consistently, precisely and with a little more effort than a six weight. The 5 or even 6 weight rod will have difficulty casting the larger air resistant flies. They will require more effort and be less pleasurable.

There are basically three different actions to choose when considering a fly rod. A rod will have a fast action, medium action or a slow action. Fast action means the rod will flex in the upper portion just towards the tip.

A medium action will be a little less stiff with a bit more

flex down the tip and a slow action will flex all the way to mid rod. The most preferred by beginner to intermediate casters is a medium flex rod. Some advanced casters like a fast or very fast action with some liking the feel of a medium action rod. It's about personal preference. Folks who predominantly fish small flies in the 16 to 24 range usually prefer the medium or slow action rod as might those who mostly fish subsurface with nymphs and streamers.

Brief Review: Choose a fly rod by the size flies to be cast and the specifics of the water body. Will you be fishing a large river with a brisk current or a smaller river with slower moving water - Small to medium pond or a larger lake? Will medium or longer casts be needed?

## Fly Reels

Fly fishermen are fortunate to have so many dependable reel choices today. Most models starting around fifty dollars will do a fine job for smallmouth. These fish are not known to make long, blistering runs. Seldom will a bass take you into the backing unless it is a big fish that worked its way into heavy current, your drag is set too loose or a combination of the two.

There are three types of fly reels – Single Action, Multiplying and Automatic. First of all stay away from Automatic Fly Reels. They do not work well and are more useful as toys for children. That brings us to the two practical types. Single Action fly reels are the most used because of their dependability. They retrieve the equivalent of one rotation of the spool with every turn of the handle. With large arbor spools they now come close in line retrieval to the Multiplying type. In those situations where it is important to retrieve line very quickly a Multiplying Fly Reel may be a good choice. They retrieve the equivalent of two, three or more rotations of the spool with every 360 degree turn of the handle. They may help a person retrieve line fast enough when hooked to a fish so as to keep slack from developing.

If you find it increasingly challenging to maintain tension on a fish after a hookup a multiplying fly reel may be the answer. (Reading the Control System Chapter may help) More internal parts are used in this model which translates to a better chance for repairs or failure during a critical time (Murphy's Law). They also weigh more.

There will be many casts involved when fly fishing for smallmouth bass. A fly reel two to three ounces heavier can make a difference for your casting arm by the end of a day. Some fly fishing anglers will argue the aesthetics of a Single Action Fly Reel is more about what the sport is supposed to be offering — a closer feel to the fish, requiring a higher degree of skill and giving greater satisfaction. Of course this will depend upon the species pursued, the conditions and personal preference.

There are basically two types of drag systems for a fly reel – A Spring & Pawl and a Disc Drag. The Spring & Pawl Drag is used in light fishing for panfish and small trout. The Disc Drag is the reel for all other types of fishing including bass, large trout, steelhead, salmon and saltwater.

Purchase a reel that will hold at least 50 yards of backing along with the fly line. Backing is 50 or more yards of Dacron or gel spun material which is tied onto all fly reels before attaching the fly line. It provides bulk so that the fly line is not as compressed into small memory causing coils. More importantly the backing provides insurance from a long running fish that may take all the fly line. (Most fly lines are usually ninety to one hundred and five feet long).

The phrase commonly associated with the use of backing is: "The fish made a long run taking me into the backing". Hence, the backing provides insurance against losing the line and fish to a long run or just running out of fly line. The correct amount of backing should be knotted onto the reel prior to tying in a fly line. The amount will depend upon the species pursued, the reels capacity and the conditions. For almost all bass situations 50 yards of backing is acceptable, 100 to 200 yards if you are also pursuing larger running fish with the same equipment.

If a reel with quality machining, a smooth dependable drag capable of long runs, reliability and pride in ownership is your desire then be prepared to pay two hundred dollars to upward of over seven hundred dollars. They are machined from a single block of aircraft aluminum and include a minimal approach using the highest quality machined internal parts. If your interest is in a reel used only for smallmouth a price of fifty to one hundred dollars will do the job with fifty yards of backing.

It is a good idea to have backing below the fly line on the reel to prevent the buildup of line memory (twists and coils) and allow a better running, more consistent drag. Install enough backing to fill the reel spool when the line is added but not too much to allow the fly line to rub the inside of the reel as the handle is turned. Fly reels are listed with the size line and amount and size of backing recommended.

Reels from the higher end will do an excellent job for smallmouth and can be used for other species such as trout, steelhead, salmon and even light saltwater. Load it with one to two hundred yards of backing attached to the reel and then to the fly line. (The amount of backing will depend upon the species pursued and conditions).

## FLY LINES FOR SMALLMOUTH

### Floating Line

A weight forward floating line is preferred when surface fishing for smallmouth. This line has most of it's weight distributed in the first 35-40 feet, followed by a thin, integrated running line. This weighting allows quick and effortless loading and casting of the rod. The best choices are an all purpose weight forward or a bass bug tapered which has a slightly beefier head. The later does a better job of casting the larger poppers, hair bugs and Dahlberg diver style flies popular with top water fishing for this species. This line will also cast the smaller poppers. Use an 8 - 10 foot tapered leader with an 8 to 12 pound tippet when fishing on or near the surface for smallmouth. The tippet size depends on the size flies used. A large air resistant popper or hair bug will cast better with a 12 pound tippet while a size 6 to 10 fly will cast well with an 8 to 10 pound tippet.

There are fly rods that will not cast a bass bug taper line well and there are some that excel when rigged with this line. Some fly rods are not beefy enough to handle this type of line but will work well with a standard weight forward or double taper. These are usually rods designed for more finesse use when pursuing smaller trout or panfish. When purchasing a rod try to cast two or three different lines to find the best casting feel and combination for your outfit.

## Sink Tips

A sink tip is really two lines used as one. It has a front sinking section integrated into a rear floating section. A leader is tied to the front sinking section. The rear floating part is tied to the backing.

Sink Tip or Sinking Lines come in different densities of a one inch sink rate per second to a nine inch sink rate per second. This type of fly line will effectively work the four to ten foot water depth range depending upon retrieve rate and line manipulations and line density (slow sinking, medium sinking, fast sinking, extra fast sinking, etc.).

My preference is for a five to six inch per second sink rate for most situations (extra fast). The 24 foot style (made popular by Jim Teeny) sink rate is determined by grains. A 150 grain is about right for a 5 or 6 weight with a 200 grain used for a 7 or 8 weight. These 24 foot sink tips will get the fly down an extra two or three feet deeper as compared to a 10 to 15 foot extra fast sink tip. The reason is the running line integrated into the sinking head is much thinner allowing the sinking portion less resistance when attaining depth.

Another option is a five foot sink tip. This line will have a closer feel to a full floating line when casting, working well for the 2 – 4 foot depth. If only one tip is purchased opt for either a five foot or 10 to 15 foot sink tip in the extra fast configuration. The other sinking tip heads are for fine tuning.

A leader for a sink tip line should be much shorter than a leader used for a floating line. The goal is to fish sub-surface. A longer leader will buoy upward in the water column and defeat the purpose of the sinking section which is to pull the leader and fly down. A longer leader hinders this. The shorter leader will follow the path of the sinking section of line as it drifts along while showing the fly to our sought-after species at the proper depth. A longer leader will not accomplish this as effectively when used with a sinking line of any type. The sinking portion of the line looses its effectiveness in forcing the leader to follow its path.

## Smallmouth Leader for Sink Tips and Sinking Lines

Tie a 10 to 12 inch section of 20 pound Maxima Chameleon to the sinking line with either a nail knot, needle knot or loop to loop if the line has one. Then tie a Surgeons loop knot onto the free end. Add another 5 to 6 inch piece of 15 pound Maxima Chameleon with surgeon loops tied on each end. To complete the leader add a 3 inch piece of 12 pound Maxima with loops on each end. Connect the loops to make an approximate 18 to 21 inch leader butt section. Next, tie on 24 to 36 inches of 4x to 2x fluorocarbon material with a Uni Knot and the fly is ready to be added. The tippet will break before the loops give out. Just add another tippet. It is a good idea to occasionally check the connections of the three section looped butt section for wear.

## Full Sinking Lines

Full sinking lines come in basically the same density rate as sink tips. The big difference is the entire line sinks. The short leader will follow the path of the line along the bottom as the sink tip. The rigging for the leader is the same as for the Sink Tip and Teeny T series Line. Usually, the retrieve is slower with a full sinking line affording a closer to the bottom presentation for a longer period of time. If the strike zone for that time of day is closer to the bottom, this method will keep the fly in that zone for an extended period offering more strikes.

When using a sinking tip or full sinking line it may become difficult to make another cast. If this occurs bring in more line, make a roll cast, one back cast and then shoot the line. For sink tips and shooting heads retrieve the line to the point where the sinking portion meets the floating portion is just a few inches past the rod tip. Make a roll cast, one back cast and then shoot the floating portion. This usually works very well because the heavier sinking portion loads the rod quickly. If you are still having difficulty bring in more of the sinking portion through the rod tip and then cast in the manner described.

## Multi Tip Lines

This is a line with a loop and four separate interchangeable head sections which are twelve to fifteen feet long with loops for attaching to the main running line. They include a floating head and three others with different sinking densities. By simply changing a looped section a person may effectively fish from the surface to a number of depths. This works great when using just one reel without spare spools. Simple yet effective. The storage case provided makes it convenient to store and change different density heads by simply connecting the loops.

This system works well however the junction where the heads attach can become a slight nuisance. It is not integrated, causing a slight interruption when necessary to work the connection through the rod tip and guides. Once enough line is through this is not an issue until it becomes necessary to work the junction through the guides again. Of course there are trade offs in any minimizing. Fishing Guides usually will have two or three rods rigged (Fly rods or spinning) enabling a change from a floater to a sinking as easy as choosing another golf club. Experienced nonguide fishermen will also set up two, three or more rods in a similar fashion.

When using one fly rod with a multi tip line there will be a need to pull over out of the current to change heads so as to not float by productive water. Fly fishing anglers who carry extra spare spools rigged with different density lines are able to change over from one to another no quicker than changing heads with a Multi Tip Line. This line is a very good option eliminating the need to purchase spare spools for different lines and is an excellent choice for the cost-conscious angler.

## FLY SELECTION

There are thousands of flies which can be used when fly fishing for smallmouth bass. The following is a list which I have had a good deal of success with. An eight to ten foot leader with a 8 - 12 pound tippet is fine for the surface.

## Surface Flies for Smallmouth

1. POPPERS – Sizes 2-10. My favorites are Gaines Dixie Devil and Gaines Dynamite In sizes 4, 6 & 8 - Color is 040 or 041. Popular Colors for Poppers– Blue, Chartreuse, Frog, Orange, and Yellow.

2. SLIDERS – Sizes 6-10 (Example – Sneaky Pete Style made of cork). Popular Colors are Yellow, Chartreuse, Orange and White.

3. DAHLBERG DIVER STYLE – Sizes 2-8 - Made of deer hair or a combination of deer hair and marabou with or without flash & rubber strips. Popular Colors: Frog, Yellow, Chartreuse, Orange, Olive, and Red, Black, White and combinations of one or more of each. My favorites colors are frog, Yellow or Chartreuse in Sizes 2 and 6.

4. DEER HAIR BUGS – Sizes 2–8. Popular Colors – Frog, Yellow, and Fruit Cocktail, plus combinations of Yellow, Orange, Red and Olive.

5. ELK HAIR CADDIS. Sizes 12–16, - Colors: Tan, olive, peacock herl and gray.

6. STIMULATOR. Sizes 8-12 . Colors: Yellow, Orange and Red.

7. TARANTULA OR MADAM X. Sizes 8-12 . Colors: Yellow, Orange and Red.

8. WULFF. Sizes 8–14. Colors: White, Royal, and Ausable.

9. HOPPERS. Yellow, Sizes 8–12, either traditional fur & feather or foam.

10. STONEFLY. Sizes 6–12, either traditional fur & feather or foam.

11. BEETLE. Sizes 10–14.

12. ANT. Sizes 12-16.

13. SURFACE MAYFLIES. Sizes 8-14.

The smaller size 12–16 flies can work well during low water and bright sunny conditions when the noisy gulp from poppers, Dahlberg Diver-style flies and hair bugs will spook fish. The Tarantula, Madam X, Stimulator, hoppers and surface stonefly solicit strikes especially well when there are stoneflies or hoppers on the water and can also be used as searching patterns. The Wulffs are good for imitating a wide variety of insects especially in size 12 or 14 during the White Fly (Ephron Leukon) hatch. A bonus when pursuing smallies is they may just take one of these flies because it represents a food item.

Most days smallmouth are not as selective as Trout. There are those times during the season that they will appear to be selective towards the larger hatches of the mid size white fly size 12 – 14 (Ephron Leukon), the Alder Fly size 14 – 16 or even a smaller Blue Winged Olive or Baetis type insects in size 18 – 22. It is amazing to see these bass feed on the smaller flies. They appear just as a trout when taking them with a subtle surface movement of their nose, dorsal, adipose fin or tail as they gorge themselves. These smaller insects are high in protein and concentrated in numbers allowing the consumption of numerous flies with each slurp. The best part is the smallmouth, because of their makeup, are not as selective as a trout would be when focused upon a particular insect or stage of an insect. Most good casts will be rewarded with a strike even if the offering is off color or size.

14. DEER HAIR MOUSE. Sizes 2–8. Natural Deer Hair color. This is a great fly for explosive top water strikes. It can be a bit air resistant to cast especially in sizes 2 and 4 but can bring up the big ones.

## Floating Line: Subsurface Flies for Smallmouth

A ten to twelve pound tippet is excellent for casting poppers, Dahlberg Divers and deer hair bugs, Mouse imitations, etc, but the heavy diameter will not allow subsurface flies to sink or fish properly when using a floating line and may spook fish unless an adjustment is made. Tie a three to six foot section of 3x - 5x (3 – 8 pound) to the floating leader (depending on conditions) to allow these flies to drop and fish correctly. This tippet can be easily cut and a top water hair bug or cork popper added if you decide to try the surface a little later.

1. CLOUSERS. Sizes 6-10. Colors: Baby Bass, Red & White, Yellow Perch, Sculpin, and Chartreuse.

2. BEAD HEAD & CONE HEAD WOOLY BUGGERS.

Sizes 6-10. My favorite colors are Black, Brown and Olive. Also try Chartreuse & White.

3. WOOLY GRUBBERS AND SCORPIONS. Sizes 4-8. Colors Brown, Black, Tan, and White.

4. RABBIT STRIP OR MARIBOU STREAMER FLIES. Sizes 4-10. Colors: Brown, Black, Olive, White and Chartreuse.

5. DEER HAIR AND MARABOU TYPE STREAMERS - Sizes 4-10.

6. MARIBOU MUDDLER. Sizes 4-10, Bead Head. Colors : Yellow, White & Black

7. ZONKERS. Sizes 4-10 Colors: White, Olive, Black and Brown.

8. CRAWFISH IMITATIONS (Non Weighted). Sizes 4-8 Colors: Brown or Olive. Drift a non weighted crawfish fly along the bottom with twitches rigged with a strike indicator and non lead split shot.
CRAWFISH IMITATIONS (Weighted). Sizes 4-8. Color Brown or Olive. These are fished with a floating line & leader with a finer tippet of 4x to 5x.

9. STONEFLY IMITATIONS (Golden, Black & Brown) Sizes 4–8. used with or without a Strike indicator and non lead split shot. These are dead drifted without action in slow to moderate current along the bottom.

10. SOFT HACKLES AND BEAD HEAD NYMPHS. These are used in low water spooky fish conditions.

They can be fished by themselves or tied onto the bend of a streamer as can a nymph. Soft Hackles and Nymphs can also be tied to the bend of any streamer fly or sub surface stonefly in the same fashion. (Such as bead head & cone head Wooly buggers or size 2 to 8 stonefly imitations) or fished sub surface by themselves with shot or shot and an indicator in slow to medium current to spooky fish. Usually when using these finesse fly fishing techniques the fish have been spotted and are visually worked with precise casts and drifts. Works especially well for spooky fish (low water or bright sunny conditions) which are not responsive to conventional methods. My favorite soft hackles are yellow floss body and partridge, olive floss body & partridge, Orange floss body and partridge, peacock herl and partridge and hares ear and partridge. Sizes 12-16 These soft hackles are also great for trout either sub surface with shot or fished without shot and swung through target areas, especially those containing showing feeding trout. A size 14-20 nymph can be added to the bend of a soft hackle with a short tippet of 6–10 inches with very good results. My favorite nymphs for smallmouth and trout are Hares Ear, Pheasant Tail, Prince & Copper John, sizes 14-20 and black or golden stonefly, sizes 4-10.

## Sink Tip Fly Selection for Smallmouth

1. WOOLY BUGGERS – Bead Head, Cone Head and Non Weighted – The choice will depend upon the depth desired and the velocity of the current. (This will be covered in the Techniques and Strategy section). Sizes 6-10. Colors: Black, Brown, Olive, White and Chartreuse.

2. WOOLY GRUBBER & SCORPION. These are similar flies to a Wooly Bugger only they have a plastic high action tail. My favorite colors are brown or chartreuse, sizes 4-8.

3. LARGE STONEFLY NYMPHS. Sizes 4-10. Colors: Golden, Black and Brown.

4. RABBIT STRIP STREAMER OR MARIBOU MUDDLER. Sizes 4-8. Colors: Black, Yellow, White and Olive.

5. ZONKERS. Sizes 4-10. Colors: Black, White, Brown, Olive and Yellow.

6. MARIBOU STREAMER. Sizes 4-0.

7. NYMPHS & SOFT HACKLES can be tied on any of the flies in this selection by simply tying one to the bend of the fly with a six to twelve inch piece of fluorocarbon as previously mentioned.

## Full Sinking Line Fly Selection
The same flies are used for this line as for the Sink Tip. Generally the retrieve is much slower allowing the fly to run very deep.

## Knots
The easiest way to learn to tie all the necessary fishing knots and also familiarize oneself with the application of each is to visit one of the best knot tying site on the internet – www.animatedknots.com. A search of "fishing knots" will offer many other very good options.

************

# Spinning Equipment for Smallmouth

## Spinning Rod

A medium light to medium power spinning rod from 5 to 7 feet feet should meet most anglers needs for small-mouth. The actions of a rod vary from slow to extra fast. The type of water to be fished should be considered when purchasing a rod.

My preference is for a fast action rod. Rods will be rated by the action and also power of the rod. They are ultra light 1-6 lb, light 4-8 lb, medium light 4-10 lb, medium 6-12 lb, medium heavy, 10-15, heavy or extra heavy power 15-50+ lb with a slow, medium, fast or extra fast action. I do not use medium heavy, heavy or extra heavy spinning rods for smallmouth fishing. There aren't any lures or plugs in my spinning arsenal for Smallmouth that weigh over a 1/2 ounce with most being 3/8 ounce or less. Four to ten pound line is used.

A fun option is a fast action, Ultra Light or Light Rod in a 5 to 6 foot length. The recommended lure weight for these rods is 1/32 to 1/4 ounce and 1/16 to 3/8 ounce. These rods are a blast for smallmouth. A river bass will feel like a monster on one. A few surface strikes may be missed with them because they do not have the backbone to set the hook as in the medium light to medium power fast or extra fast action rods. Still, most who fish lighter rods feel this is part of the challenge to overcome and have a lot of fun with it. They may not be the right tool for the job in every situation but provide great entertainment value when used. Two to six pound line is used with them.

The price paid for a smallmouth rod can run $25. and up. A $25 spinning rod will do the job, but sad to say, a rod with a sensitive feel, lighter quality materials and better workmanship which will offer longevity will cost a bit more. Examine several rods before purchasing. I like a fast action rod with medium light to medium power for most surface work, tubes, jigs, worms and crankbaits. For shallow to mid depth running Rapalas, and smaller diving plugs use an ultra light or light fast action rod. If you do use larger crankbaits or spinnerbaits 3/4 ounce or larger a medium heavy rod of 6 to 7 feet is recommended.

## Spinning Reel

Most spinning reels costing $25 and up will do a nice job for smallmouth. They should last at least a couple of seasons, depending on amount of use and abuse. The higher priced ones will last longer, offer better quality with a smoother drag. I have never purchased a spinning reel for more than $75. I am sure they are wonderful but the more expensive models are not for me. (Numerous high end spinning reels are now running in the $300 to $700 Range). I like to place my money where it will give the most benefit. I believe those jewels are not really needed for smallmouth but then again, that depends on personal preference and pride in ownership. Purchase the best which is affordable to you.  Most companies offer discounts for purchasing a rod and reel together.  Yes, Walmart and Kmart do have fair to good equipment for very good prices.  They do not carry the higher end.

I like a spinning reel that will hold at least 100 yards of the chosen line and has a smooth drag under pressure with no jerky slips when tested.  My preference is for one that has a click adjustment drag either on the face or base.  This allows for precise, repeatable drag adjustments.

## Line

Recommended lines for the recreational spinning smallmouth angler should be from four to ten pounds. The super lines, also referred to as braided lines have far more pluses going for them than negatives. They have thinner diameter, allowing deeper running and faster dropping of offerings, larger line capacity for the reel, more sensitive feel and do not develop memory as easily as monofilament.

Change any mono line less than 8 pounds that has been used for more than two or three trips. I have lost too many fish because of weakened line. My guests work hard to hook up with their fish. I do not wish to lose one because of using line with questionable integrity.

Lighter monofilament line will develop memory and lose strength quickly. It will decrease in integrity after playing a fish or two. Always cut off several feet of line and retie after playing a couple of fish or a large, hard fighting one if using 6 pound test or less. Check the line for abrasions every several casts or after a hang up or coming through heavy cover.

Braided Line can and often does hold up for a whole season. The knots and tangles usually come out much easier than with mono. However, when you do experience a deep tangle with braid a lot of line can be lost.

These super lines cast excellently. The down side is they will not accept the improved clinch knot well. Two good and easy to tie knots which do work for braided line are the Uni Knot (Duncan Loop) and the Surgeon's Loop.

Another issue to be aware of is to be very careful when handling the super braids. Because of high strength with such small diameter, this line will quickly cut into your hands. For an example, beware if there is a lure or plug hung in a tree, on the bank or on the bottom. Do not retrieve the line and lure by wrapping a couple of loops around your hand and pulling especially if floating on a river.

Braided line can be used by itself when working the surface with excellent results but I believe adding a 3 - 6 foot tippet section of 4 - 8 pound fluorocarbon with a Uni Knot or Surgeons Loop for subsurface presentations will  bring more strikes.  There is a price to pay for technology.  Braided lines average five times as much in cost as premium monofilament.

When using mono I like to opt for a slightly stiffer line instead of the soft and supple type when using 6 pound test or less.  The reason for this is I have not found a softer mono which does not develop memory to the point of becoming a nuisance in the lower weights. Although soft  mono casts exceptionally well, too much time is spent untying knots or trying to remove memory twists or tangles when using lighter weights.  This is especially true with guests who do not have the daily experience of handling and casting a line with these characteristics.  By offering clients the use of a quality, slighter stiffer mono, I am able to keep them participating in the game instead of spending fishing time untying knots.

## Spinning Offerings for Smallmouth

### Surface Plugs – Basic Selection:

FROG, SOFT PLASTIC  Size: 3-5 inch.

REBEL POP-N-R   Colors: Bass, Silver & Black, Rainbow, and Yellow Perch.  Sizes – 1/8 ounce & 1/4 ounce.

HEDDON BABY & TINY TORPEDO   Colors: Perch & Natural Bullfrog.

ZARA SPOOK  Colors: Rainbow, Natural Bullfrog, and Perch. Size: Puppy.

## Surface to Four Feet Subsurface – Basic Selection:

FLOATING RAPALA  Fishes well from the surface to 3 feet subsurface.  Colors: Rainbow, Gold, Silver, and Perch. Size: 7 and 9.

SINKING RAPALA  Fishes well 3-5 feet subsurface. Colors: Rainbow, Gold, Silver, and Perch. Sizes: 3 -7.

RAPALA X RAP  Fishes well 3-5 feet sub surface. Colors: Silver/Red and Natural Green.

REBEL CRAWFISH Fishes well 3-5 feet subsurface (depending on size). Colors: Brown and  Olive.

SPINNER BAIT  Effective 1-8 feet subsurface depending upon retrieve. Colors:  Chartreuse, Yellow, and White. Size: 1/8 - 3/8 ounce.  Different blade choices are Willow Leaf, the Rounder Colorado and Indiana.

The following deep divers can cover water 4 to 10 feet depending upon size:

## Diving Crank Baits and Jerk Baits – Basic Selection:

LUHR JENSEN SPEED TRAP  Colors: Perch, Crawfish, any familiar baitfish color.

RAPALA JOINTED SHAD RAP  Colors: Silver, Crawfish, and Yellow Perch.

Rapala Husky Jerkbait  Colors: Gold, Silver, and Perch.

## Soft Plastics – Basic Selection:

SENKOS  Can be fished weightless texas rigged, texas rigged with weight, weightless wacky style, and drop shot with weight. Colors: Black with Blue or Red Glitter, Green Pumpkin,  Pearl,  or Watermelon with Red Flake. Size: 5 inch, 6 inch.

TUBES  Usually fished with 1/16 to 1/2 oz. weight. Colors: Chartreuse, Natural Crawfish, Green Pumpkin, Pearl, White, Smoke, and Watermelon with Red Flake.

FLUKES  Fished weightless Texas Rigged or Texas Rigged with weight.  May also be Carolina Rigged or drop shot.  There is a slot for the hook. Colors: White Ice, Baby Bass,  or Arkansas Shiner. Size:  3 - 6 inch. There are other companies who produce products similar to the Fluke series. They all work and can catch smallmouth from top to bottom depending on the retrieve or if weight is attached.

## Picture Taking Help

The introduction of digital cameras made it wonderfully convenient to share quality outdoor pictures through emails and on DVDs and CDs.  Because catch and release is practiced by most smallmouth anglers it is very important to try and omit additional stress to the fish we are going to release after enjoying them. A Boga Grip or similar device is the perfect tool for picture taking. They conveniently and firmly attach to the mouth offering less stress and a better chance for survival. There is little or no handling necessary with the chance of dropping nearly eliminated.

I became adamant about this because on several occasions guests lost control of a fish while posing for a picture causing them to bounce off the floor of the boat. Upon release their survival was questionable. These beautiful creatures who gave their hearts in battle deserve better.

The Boga Grip is a quality built item designed to last a lifetime. They run around one hundred and twenty dollars which is a bit expensive but still a good investment. There are similar types available by other companies for less money.

## Resources:

BOGA GRIP - estabogagriptackle.com
BASS PRO GRIP MASTER – basspro.com
BERKELEY LIP GRIP TOOLS – www.berkley-fishing.com
CABELAS GRAB + WEIGH – cabelas.com
RAPALA LOCK N WEIGH – rapala.com

*************

# Watercraft and Boat Handling

Renting will be the best option if casually paddling a canoe or kayak a time or two a season. Most liveries for a fee offer shuttle service with canoe rentals. You will need only one vehicle. First contact them prior to your outing with a date and time and deposit arrangements. They will provide a craft or crafts, paddles, life jackets (pfd), and shuttle service to the launch site, usually upriver. Make sure to ask about shuttle service if you need it. Your vehicle is left at their place. At the end of the float the rented canoe or kayak will be left there and you simply drive away in your car. This is how most liveries operate. If different they will inform you.

The rental fees for a day range from $60 - $90. per canoe for two including shuttle service and $40 - $60 without. Bring a fishing rod, binoculars, lunch and a few personal items to enjoy a terrific, inexpensive outing.

Another option is to use a flat bottom Jon Boat (12 - 20 foot ) with an electric motor. Rig this with a pair of oars and you have the ability to pin point row through runs and class one or two rapids while returning to the electric motor for the flatter areas or if an in your face wind develops. Of course, if you desire to return or motor upstream a gas motor may be needed if the current velocity present makes it necessary. A jet motor or prop guard is a good idea if navigating a rocky shallow river. This depends on the river and the specific personal wants and needs to navigate your river comfortably, effectively and safely.

## Resource: Flat Bottom Boats:
LOWE BOATS - loweboats.com
LUND BOATS - lundboats.com
TRACKER BOATS – trackerboats.com

## Resource: Jet Sleds & Boats
FISH RITE BOATS - fish-rite.com
KOFFLER BOATS - kofflerboats.com
RB BOATS – rbboats.com
Willie Boats – willieboats.com

## Square Back Canoes
They offer good stability and even better when equipped with stabilizer pontoons. These pontoons (purchased at Cabelas) easily attach to the sides of the canoe and extend into the water. The Coleman Scanoe

or Pelican Bayou Canoe is the same model. Both are 16 feet 3 Inches long, 43 inches wide and made of a tough Ram X fiberglass material and have a capacity of 950 pounds. This boat is great for two with some gear. It will accept up to a 5 HP gas motor. An electric motor may be a better option depending on your needs. This craft can be transported either on a small trailer, tied down in the back of a pickup truck on top of your vehicle with a canoe tie down kit.

The Grumman Square Back Canoe is 19 feet long, offers room for 3, has a capacity of 1100 pounds along with a 40 1/8 inch bottom. It is more expensive but offers a bigger boat design for larger payloads. This canoe is well made and used by many professionals. This craft can be transported on a light duty canoe carrier or on top of a vehicle with a canoe carrying kit with care. Its size make this canoe awkward to handle out of the water.

## Canoe or Kayak

Canoes and Kayaks open up a whole new world of possibilities for a person or two wanting to float a river either to fish or experience a scenic adventure. They are relatively inexpensive compared to other alternatives and are easily transported on top of a vehicle with a tie down kit. I do recommend for beginners to add clip on pontoons to insure a safe and worry free float.

Make sure to have a properly rated life jacket for each person before beginning a float. Scout the river ahead visually throughout the float making sure to make paddling adjustments well before challenging sections. Do not allow a canoe or kayak to turn sideways through shallow sections or areas with increased current. They tip over very easily if the bottom is dragged when passing through shallow gravel bars, riffs and rapids when positioned sideways. The slightest rubbing of the river bottom will do it. Give bank hugging blow downs and low overhanging shoreline tree and brush branches a wide path.

When float fishing a river with a canoe the standard protocol is for one person to fish at a time while the other maintains boat control. In set backs and areas away from the main flow of the current this may not be necessary but for the most part it will be.
Listed are a few of the popular canoe resources. There are numerous purveyors of kayaks. Listed are a few of them.

## Resource: Canoes
COLEMAN SQUARE BACK CANOE - made of Ram X material - coleman.com
PELICAN SQUARE BACK BAYOU CANOE - dickssportinggoods.com
GRUMMAN 19 FOOT SQUARE BACK CANOE - marathonboat.com
MOHAWK CANOE – mohawkcanoe.com
MAD RIVER CANOE – madrivercanoe.com
OLD TOWN CANOE – www.oldtowncanoe.com

## Resource: Kayaks
HERITAGE KAYAKS – heritagekayaks.com
HOBIE – hobiecat.com
L.L. BEAN – llbean.com
NATIVE WATERCRAFT – nativewatercraft.com
WILDERNESS KAYAKS – wildernesssystems.com

## Inflatable Pontoon Boat

Some folks enjoy more hands on. A one or two person inflatable pontoon boat may be just the ticket for you. Purchase one as a package and it will come with oars, oar locks, frame, storage side bags rear cargo deck, etc.

Some models can easily handle up to class three and even class four rapids. They are fairly easy to set up after the first couple of practice sessions. Purchase a craft at least eight feet long with angled upward tubes for floating a river. The better models are made of long wearing quality materials with a 5 to 10 year warranty. Consider only a quality model for floating a river.

You will need to wear stocking foot waders with wading shoes or shorts with sandals or sneakers. Flippers are optional but walking will be difficult with them making it very easy to lose balance or fall. I prefer to use oars with stocking foot waders and wading shoes when operating this type of craft.

### Resource: Pontoon Boats

DAVE SCADDEN PONTOON BOAT - northforkout-doors.com
PONTOON BOATS - Cabelas.com
OUTCAST SPORTING GEAR - www.outcastboats.com
THE RIVER MAN - theriverman.com

## McKenzie Drift Boats

These boats are used by professionals as well as many recreational outdoor enthusiasts. A person who purchases a drift boat and uses it often will find staying in top shape is inevitable. These are for those enthusiasts who enjoy exercising for long periods especially when you find yourself on a huge pool or flat with a head-wind. You can experience less rowing with this option if an electric or small gas motor is added. These boats open up an option for guiding or just becoming popular with friends. They are the ultimate in becoming one with the river.

Drift boats will not only reach all the best fishing spots on a river but when operated properly can handle rapids up to and including class 3 safely. They offer a comfortable, Cadillac-like alternative for floating a river.

The choice in drift boats are aircraft aluminum, wood or fiberglass - high side or low side. My preference is for aluminum because of the way they ride on and in the water compared to those made from fiberglass or wood, the lack of upkeep necessary and the abuse they are able to withstand. I have rowed all three. My preference is for a high side model because they provide better security and a safer feeling for my guests and are able to navigate larger rapids while keeping my guests dry. After rowing each, it is my belief aluminum is more durable, safer, rides better, rows very well, slides as easy or better and is as quiet if fitted with a UHMW bottom. This material consists of lightweight 1/10th to 1/8th inch thick polymer sheets which are applied to the entire boat bottom using an adhesive or riveting method. UHMW provides a "greasy", slick-when-wet body of armor which provides extra protection for the hull bottom while enabling the boat to slide more easily over gravel and rocks.

Because I am a fishing guide wood is not an option.

They are beautiful and run well but they need too much constant upkeep for my purposes. I do not want to shudder each time someone spills a drink or a rock is bumped.

Overall, I feel this particular choice contributes to my guests feeling much safer, enabling them a feeling of well being throughout their float trip experience with me. This is a personal preference from one fishing guide's perspective. There are some professionals who prefer and use fiberglass or wood drift boats.

An experienced drift boat or raft operator reacts instinctively with great efficiency and seemingly little thought to river challenges. Although it appears a guide is living the moment with you while offering fishing suggestions when needed, they have many more responsibilities. One of these is viewing the river and planning rowing adjustments two or three steps ahead.

An important basic rule when going over a shallow shoal is always keep the boat headed straight or angled 45 degrees and not fully sideways. If negotiating fully sideways the velocity of the current may push over the craft if it hangs up on gravel or hits a rock just below the surface. At the very least the boat will come to a sudden stop with the possibility of ejecting a passenger. When traveling straight downstream the boat will slide along until depth is reached even if the boat drags bottom. There may be a need to get out and push or drag the boat a little if you miss the slot and hang up but that would be the worst that could happen. In all but very shallow areas a 45 degree angle is acceptable when navigating through. A swipe or two just before with one oar while lifting the other will bring the boat to a straight position for traveling through the very shallow places.

Most of the time rowing will be spent pushing with the oars instead of pulling with the bow facing down-stream or in the general downstream direction. This, with the current is how to move downstream. Pulling with both or one oar allows you to set the angle and is used in conjunction with pushing for making adjust-ments while traveling downstream.

Combine these all together and a drift boat operator can easily navigate almost anywhere in a river system allowing their guests fishing opportunities not attain-able from other craft.

Always face downstream with the bow first. In this manner, all can be seen, set up and reacted to ahead of time. When finding yourself in close quarters with a brisk current point the bow in the direction you do not want to go, then pull away with a series of oar strokes. Do not try and push through in this scenario until you own the experience to differentiate between navigating issues. It is better to overcompensate by setting up too early than to not negotiate in time and find yourself wrapped around a boulder or tipped over by a huge blow down or large overhanging tree or protruding branch near shoreline current.

A brisk current will work through a downed tree with limbs exposed above the surface, pulling most craft in the same direction. When this occurs, the currents velocity will push or pull the boat through the obstruction. This is one of the few easy to avoid and dangerous situations not to find yourself in.

Position the boat to pull away instead of pushing through in this situation. For some reason most beginner drift boat operators want to push through instead of pulling away. Remember this and it may save you from a dangerous and embarrassing moment. Point the bow towards the direction you do not want to go, then pull away. Maintain a 45 to 70 degree angle as you do. It may take a few strokes or even five or six before the boat begins to respond. Stay with it and the boat will react to your rowing, leaving a safe margin. Do not wait until the last second to set up. Perceive and prepare for river challenges ahead before finding yourself in the middle of one. You will develop a feel for how and when to react to each different situation encountered after navigating a few. Set up for river challenges earlier than necessary especially when still learning. This will give you the room to operate safely until more experienced.

Pulling gives better control than pushing. By pulling with the right oar and lifting the left together the boat will pivot to the right. If you pull with the left oar and lift the right the boat will pivot to the left. By pulling with both oars the boat will move straight.

If you wish to quickly turn left pull with the left oar while pushing with the right. If a quick right turn is desired pull with the right oar while pushing with the left. Practice and this will become second nature.

Develop your expertise safely with these different oar

strokes in a slow moving river section or even a pond. This will help you to gain the skills to properly steer the boat. Once this is accomplished, navigating a drift boat is as easy as steering a car with perhaps just a little more work from the operator. Line the boat up with the desired angle then pull away with a series of strokes. After this is accomplished bring the boat in line and casually begin pushing or pulling with the oars again. If you wish to hold position or move upstream pull with both oars.

In very shallow water (2 to 6 inches) keep the boat straight. If you are sure the water is deep enough the angle of the boat doesn't matter as long as it is at the best angle for your guests to cast and the wind is not too brisk and your load is properly balanced.

I witnessed a guide and his drift boat tip over during windy conditions on New York's Salmon River. The air temp was in the low forties with 6 inches of snowfall the night before. The boat was drifting downriver sideways through a rapid with a brisk wind blowing downstream. The front passenger was leaning on the downstream side. The boat scraped bottom and over they went. Ejected.

In a shallow water situation, where your oars cannot make an effective stroke without hitting bottom, there will be different challenges. Take three times as many quick, short, shallow, strokes to maintain control. Row with a much quicker cadence. Use short shallow strokes. Try not to bang the river bottom with the oar tips. No problem. Control the craft in this manner until deeper water is reached which will again enable the oars to dig a little deeper.

Do not allow a full sideways position unless there is very little wind with minimal current velocity and your familiarity with the area ensures there is enough depth and no chance for hitting a rock or dragging bottom. Because of the design of a drift boat, it is very desirable to limit the time spent drifting sideways.

When navigating through very scratchy sections, I like to run at more of a 70 to 90 degree angle where adjustments can be made safely. If an obstruction is struck there is little danger.

Do not dig your oars much deeper than the blade width, even in deeper water. When digging the oars deep and pulling hard energy is not used efficiently. The largest benefit of boat movement in regard to energy expended will be afforded when with each oar stroke the oars are barely covered with water. Operating a drift boat is not about 20 or 30 hard strokes then a pause or a brief speed up of hard rowing and then a stop. Rowing a drift boat or raft is about making hundreds or even thousands of strokes throughout the day in an energy efficient manner. If you find yourself in a situation where it is necessary to dig the oars in a little deeper to slow the boat down or maneuver quickly, go right ahead. Safety is first and foremost. Next time try to set up a little earlier. Make the necessary adjustments as needed but remember always provide yourself plenty of room to react to challenges by setting up for maneuvers ahead of time.

When operating a McKenzie Drift Boat there are usually two fishermen, one fore and one aft. The rower is seated in the center. It is important to operate this craft safely and smoothly. Negotiate transitions from rapid to run, flat to pool to shallow areas and then parallel slow moving banks in a way that does not alter your guests casting rhythm.

Their attention need only be directed towards casting to productive areas while manipulating flies or plugs in a way which makes them more appealing. An operators job is to put them in good positions to safely accomplish this all day long, time and time again, without abrasive distractions.

A pontoon boat or raft will draft less enabling running in shallower water and will bounce off of boulders and rocks with no damage and very little disruption. For my needs a drift boat works fine because guests can stand up much more comfortably and safely with more stability. The drift boat also rows easier because there isn't any give. I also haven't any fear about puncturing any tubes when guiding spinning anglers.

Every part of work effort efficiently goes into propelling a hard chinned drift boat whereas a raft absorbs a bit of the rowers energy. This is also partly true with fiberglass boats which do not possess the hard lines of a drift boat made with aircraft grade aluminum.

## Drift Boat Builders:
### Aluminum: In alphabetical order
FISH CRAFT - theriverman.com
FISH RITE - fishrite.com
HYDE - hydeoutdoors.com

KOFFLER - kofflerboats.com
RB BOATS - rbboats.com
RIVER CRAFT DRIFT BOATS - rivercraftboats.com
RIVER WOLF DRIFT BOATS - riverwolfboats.com
SMITH ROCK RIVER BOATS - the riverman.com
WILLIE BOATS - willieboats.com

**Fiberglass Drift Boat Builders:**
HYDE - hydeoutdoors.com
CLACKACRAFT - clackacraft.com
RO - rodriftboats.com

## Wooden Drift Boat Builders:
RAYS RIVER DORIES - raysriverdories.com
TATMAN DRIFT BOATS - mckenzieriverdriftboat.com

## Inflatable Raft or Cataraft
These inflatable boats will handle much more serious
water than a drift boat. They will (unless floating class
4 or higher) easily float over an object or bounce off of
one. A drift boat will absorb the full blunt of a strike in
heavy rapids. That is why only experienced drift boat
operators should find themselves in water above class
2. Recommend reading is Neale Streek's book, *Drift
Boat Strategies*. Go with an experienced operator at
least a couple of times before attempting to run a river
with questionable rapids..

There are a few guide schools that teach the skills necessary to head you in the right direction to become
accomplished handling a drift boat or raft in moving
water. I recommend anyone with limited experience
who has purchased or acquired a drift boat, inflatable
raft or pontoon boat to attend one of these schools

unless the services of a professional operator or competent drift boat handler is available.

## Resource:

AARDVARK OUTFITTERS – aardvardoutfitters.com
Farmington, Maine
COLUMBINE FLY FISHERS – columbinefishers.com
Colorado Springs, Colorado

When a raft, cataraft or one of two man pontoon is used as a fishing boat safely, a frame and a few other items must be added. The operation of each is similar to a drift boat with a few additional benefits.

An inflatable will draft less and bounce off boulders and rocks with little disruption and no damage. I do not take guests in water over Class 3 so this is not an issue for my service. For my needs a drift boat works fine because guests can stand more comfortably and safely with more stability. The drift boat rows easier because there isn't any give. Every part of work effort is applied to propelling a hard chinned boat.

A raft will need to be inflated and deflated each time it is used unless a trailer is purchased ($1000 - $2000.) which depends on size of raft and quality of the trailer.

A drift boat or quality raft require a good sized financial investment along with an commitment of future time and energy. The cost of a new drift boat can run from six to twelve thousand dollars depending on the size, model and extras. There are many accessories available with a drift boat purchase - each adding to the total cost.

The best deal if purchasing a new McKenzie Drift Boat is to opt for a package with the extras needed included. Be aware that extras are ala carte, each adding to the total cost of the boat. In some instances the extras can be as much as the boat.

The price for a newly rigged raft or cataraft set up for fishing will be from four to over eight thousand dollars. Both a drift boat and rafting package can be purchased for considerably less if used. Ebay usually has a used assortment open to bidding. Most drift boat builders and raft dealers will have used boats (taken as trade for a new boat purchase) for sale. This type of boat is not for everyone but the rewards are high for the right type of person.

## Rafts and Rafting Supplies:
### In Alphabetical Order
CLAVEY – www.clavey.com
DOWN RIVER EQUIPMENT – downriverequip.com
NRS - nrsweb.com
RIVER CONNECTION – riverconnection.com
STAR INFLATABLES - starinflatables.com
THE RIVER MAN – theriverman.com

Be considerate of others when floating. Purchasing a fishing license and then renting or buying a boat does not give you the green light to detract from another persons outdoor experience. Basically, try to treat others as you would like to be treated if in their situation.

First and foremost when floating a river do not cut off another boat with your craft and begin fishing for any reason. The other boat has established position. This type of action demonstrates poor etiquette and character. Perhaps, if it is so important to cut in front of another boat an earlier starting time might be considered for the next outing. Quality time outdoors is a valuable commodity for everyone.

Wait a few minutes for distance to develop between you and the boat in front and then follow or cross the river. Relax, have a drink and chat. If this option is unsatisfactory give a wide birth and pass while respecting the water the other boat is casting to. Do not set up on the same side for at least a quarter mile otherwise follow the first boat leaving a comfortable distance between the two.

While in a boat, respect the water shore anglers are fishing making sure not to cast too close. They have limited access while the boating angler has the whole river. This helps to ensure a quality outdoor experience for all while demonstrating proper river etiquette. They will appreciate your kind gesture and you will feel better about yourself.

Two vehicles are needed to float a river on your own unless someone rides a bicycle or motor scooter to where the boat is launched. This is because a vehicle and trailer need to be at the end of the float to load the boat. What I usually do is first launch and then set up the boat for the day's fishing, then driving 8 miles down stream, with my truck and trailer to where the float trip will end. I meet guests here, leave my truck and trailer then drive back to the boat in their vehicle. We leave their vehicle in the parking area at the boat launch. When the float is completed the clients are given a  ride back to their vehicle.

## Boat Check List

The following is a check list viewed before each daily float with my drift boat.  I do not use a gas motor therefore gas and check oil are not on my check list.  Be sure to tell someone where you are going and approximate time of return.

Anchor & Rope
Boat Net
Boga Grip
Camera
Cell Phone
Check Guests Licenses
Drain Plug
Electric Motor & Battery if a Windy Day is Expected or Bad Weather
Extra Ball Caps
Extra Dry Clothes in Water Proof Bag
Extra Keys
Extra Tapered Leaders
Extra Winch & Strap
First Aid Kit
Fishing License
Flash Light
Flatware, Food, Grill, Ice, Folding Table, Table Cloth
Flies
Fly Floatant
Food
Forceps, Scissors & Scissor Pliers
Insect Repellent
Life Jackets Lunch – Coolers, Charcoal, Chairs, Condiments, Dishes,
Oars & Oar Locks

Rain Gear
Rods & Reels – Fly
Rods & Reels – Spinning
Sharp Knife
Spinning Lures, Plugs & Soft Baits
Split Shot
Strike Indicators
Sun Block
Sun Glasses
Tippet Material – Assorted Line Weights
Vest
Waders
Water, Drinks & Snacks
Zinger

## Raft or Cataraft Check List:
The following basic items will be needed:
Anchor & Line
Coolers & Beverage
Extra Change of Dry Clothes in Waterproof Bag
First Aid Kit
Hat
Life Jackets (PFD)
Oars & Locks
Patch Kit
Pumps - Use a Manual or Electric to inflate.  Bring a
Manual Pump along.
Fishing Frame including Casting Platforms & Thigh
Braces
Rain Gear
Seats
Straps & Tie Downs
Trailer – Gives the option of keeping the boat inflated –
Costly but convenient.

# Dam Releases

A river which is dependent upon dam releases provides different challenges or benefits than one that does not. A river without dam releases presents the fisherman with two concerns instead of three. They are river conditions and weather conditions. It is important to find out the releases every day a float is scheduled for those rivers that do have them. Most dams supply this information by phone, online or both. The dams which influence the water I float are on my favorite places on the computer. I simply click on the site for the daily releases. Most of the time this info will be accurate but there are times the actual releases may be different from what is posted. Be aware of this especially for safety reasons.

Different releases will have a different effect on the feeding activity of they bass and for most any species. Dams release from over the top, through the bottom or somewhere towards the middle. The coldest water is delivered through a bottom release. Those dams which offer high percentage bottom releases will substantially lower the river water temperature for the first mile or two presenting an excellent opportunity for trout and a good one for smallmouth bass.

The positive impact is felt most during the warmer months of the year. The release will lower the water temperature towards a more comfortable temperature for the fish (two to three degrees will make a difference) for as many as 20 to 30 miles below as well as providing an increase in oxygen. The habitat becomes better suited for smallmouth as we move downstream from the dam with trout concentrations (if trout are present in the river) holding in heavily oxygenated areas such as riffle, rapid and runs, near or up in entering streams and brooks, springs, deeper pools and shaded areas with deep water close by.

The cooler water of a bottom release dam will support a large insect base with a high percentage of smaller insects (size 18 to 24). The river will support many different insect species and sizes as we move downstream.

Approaching weather fronts can affect the feeding activity of our smallmouth. A large CFS (cubic feet per second) water release will still present feeding opportunities near structure or the shoreline away from the main current flow or in quiet water set backs. This large release along with a substantial approaching front will make for difficult fishing. Day in and day out experience allows me to make this statement.

Many dams have several large fluctuations in its releases throughout a 24 hour period. We should know the size of a dams release beforehand for the water we wish to navigate, any changes in them and how they will effect the rivers flow. This will assist towards safety as well as helping in the pursuit of our sought after fish species.

The smallmouth will adapt to the increase or decrease in water flow. Knowing releases ahead of time will enable us to react to the rivers changes, the increase or decrease in current velocity and the approximate holding positions of the bass and their prey. Smallmouth will not need to adjust their position as often below dams with smaller changes in their CFS releases.

It is imperative to be aware of how long it will take the release to reach and have an influence on the water you fish. This is accomplished by knowing how many miles per hour the release travels before it reaches your position. Go to a familiar position on the river downstream of the dam release. If you are 7 miles downstream and it takes 3 hours from the posted time of release to notice a difference in the level, velocity or clarity of the water then the release moves at 2 miles per hour.

Focus on a rock or piece of grass or brush barely above the waters surface. When this becomes covered with water, the release has reached your position. If you are

6 miles downstream and it takes 3 hours, then the release moves at 2 miles per hour.

At the beginning of the season the releases have a less positive effect except when fishing for spawning bass (Less water is more desirable). When the river is low and the water temps are up the dam releases have a greater impact upon smallmouth feeding behavior. The spring thaw in late March and early April will keep the river up thru to early May. This is the seasonal time dams releases here can exceed 35,000 CFS. That is a lot of water – over a quarter million gallons each second.

More reasonable consistent water releases should begin by early May. This will range from small minimal flow to a larger release during different periods of the day. Basically, the dams receive a higher payment during certain periods called peak power demands. They will try to run more water at these times so as to receive as much money as possible from the power generated. The different amounts of water released will have an effect on the feeding activity with certain places of the river producing better during larger releases.

During summer low water the fish will be more difficult to approach. Try to make casts a little longer to hide your presence. Once a fish becomes aware of your presence chances will decrease for a strike. It is always nice to spot a fish before casting to it but during low water conditions more success can be expected by fishing productive looking water rather than approach too closely.

Bottom line: cast a little longer according to the river

conditions and fish holding and prowling areas. This is not springtime spawning where the fish are preoccupied and more tolerant of your presence.

The creatures that live in this water must adapt to the many river and weather changes in order to survive and best take advantage of feeding opportunities while remaining safe and comfortable. During summertime low precipitation and minimal flow periods the water is warmer with less oxygen. This makes the fish less active. They are cold blooded creatures. Their temperature is the temperature of the water. There is a need to feed less when the temperature of the water is too cold or to warm. Generally this is true when water temperature is below 50 and above 79 and especially evident when dropping to the low to mid forties and above eighty).

Before the release, creatures smallmouth feed upon are able to take refuge in the low water areas which the bass are not able to access.

The dam release brings cooler water with a higher level of oxygen. Now the bass are becoming active and begin to think about eating. They are more comfortable and can breathe easier. If they were in a non active mode before the release there is a good chance when the cooler oxygenated water reaches their position neutral or active fish will be available. A degree or two can make a difference. An active fish will move twenty or thirty feet to feed, a neutral fish up to ten, and non active fish only a foot or two.

All the areas which were inaccessible or accessible with

difficulty to a smallmouth, available only to the prey they feed upon such a chubs, crawfish, minnows, dace, sculpins and insects are now prime hunting territory. In areas of the river which a few minutes before presented only inches of water are now two to three feet underwater. This is not the first time a release has presented the smallmouth in your river with a feeding opportunity. They are very proficient in taking advantage of this appreciated opportunity. It is what they do.

I try to time the releases to place my guest in those areas known to hold good populations of smallmouth bass as the influence of the release reaches that position. It's all good - The cooling water from the release, the abundant foodmass moving about helplessly, the availability of prey which had been inaccessible, the increased oxygen enabling easier breathing and rejuvenation. They are now on the bite. This can last from an hour to five or six hours. Much depends on how big the release is, for how long, water temp, weather conditions, previous conditions, etc. Is there a large amount of insect mass, baitfish or crawfish overtaken by the increased current?

These clues will present themselves if you observe the edges of current lanes and seams just below the surface. If the release is too big our quarry will not be able to fully take advantage of food swept downstream from the blunt of the increased currents velocity except in set backs, quiet bank water, seams, above and below obstructions and other areas of decreased current. These are the places to cast during the larger releases.

For best results, I prefer releases which do not present

us with a huge change in the current. The desired release is one which turns the smallmouth on, redistributes the prey they feed upon making them more easily available but does not offer challenges to negotiate the increased velocity for the smallmouth.

We want a release which gives enough increase in depth to create a movement of panic amongst prey but one that a smallmouth can easily navigate.

Another benefit of knowing when a dam is to release and how much is when a heavy rain falls the day or night before. When this occurs the chances are good the river will stain with a large release. Staining puts fish off the bite.

If a release travels at two miles an hour and the boat launch is six miles below the dam the stained water will reach our position in three to three and a half hours. If there is another launch eight to nine miles below that gives us an additional four hours before the stained water reaches that position. This knowledge can benefit us if we receive a heavy rain the day or night before with the releases during that period small. When the dam begins its larger releases the following day the river will likely stain.

A float started just six miles below the dam would have to endure the challenges of stained water conditions in about three hours after an increase in releases if a heavy rain occurred the night or day before. This depends on the amount of the release, the starting time and rain amount. Experienced fishermen here will begin further below the dam to afford themselves more time before the releases stained water reaches their position.

A dam release travels between two and two and a half miles per hour. I do not believe this will fluctuate from one river to the next except in an abrupt drop in elevation or extreme releases or flood conditions.

As stated earlier, dam releases can and often do have an effect on the feeding activity of smallmouth bass and other species. A detriment would be when a heavy rain occurs and stained water is delivered with the release or it is too large. This will drastically slow down the feeding activity of the smallmouth and force them into specific locations. These fish can be caught.

The smallmouth are affected by the suspended solids in the water column causing the brownish color of a river out of shape. This is soil washout from the surrounding area which finds its way into the river. It can be delivered from drainage ditches, brooks, streams, smaller rivers feeding into the main river and dam releases. The culprit is not enough grasses, trees and plants to hold the soil in place along with previous soil erosion. A river which stains quickly usually has been developed heavily along its banks or drainage area with too many trees and plants removed and not enough replaced.

The prey of smallmouth will seek cover, become inactive and in essence make themselves unavailable until the water begins to clear. This also changes the feeding activity of our sought-after species. Because the bass have to work harder to filter the suspended solids through their gills when breathing as well as there being less available prey to feed upon, their feeding activity level decreases until more desirable river conditions return.

This staining will continue with the releases on the Connecticut River below Wilder Dam for two to five days after a heavy rain depending on the release and if any additional precipitation occurs during the period. Each river is unique and the amount of water released will have a different effect but there are similarities between river systems.

If a release from Wilder Dam remains at 1500 or lower the water will clear after a heavy rain in a couple of days. A release of 10,000 CFS or larger will stain the river for a week. On the other side of the coin a minimal flow release of 800 CFS will find the river clear in a day or two.
Smaller rivers or upper sections of a river may call 800 CFS a large release.

Before going further, I will try to give you an idea of just how much water is being released with the rated CFS method. A cubic foot of water is approximately 7.8 gallons. When a dam releases 1000 CFS that equates to 7,800 gallons per second.

I had a float scheduled with a longtime friend and guest last season when the river here was running like chocolate milk from heavy rains. It would be a week before she would start to clear. However, 125 miles to the north the same Connecticut River was running clear and fishing well for trout. Wilder Dam was releasing 15,000 CFS yet Murphy Dam 140 miles upriver was running at 500 CFS. What a contrast. The same good sized river here is a large stream there.

My guests decided to try for trout on the upper river. It was the finest two days of trout fishing I have experienced with guests. They landed over one hundred trout from 12 to 24 inches in those two days. We lost count of how many were lost. We have also experienced the same situation in reverse - Heavily stained water on the upper river while great conditions prevailed to the south. Get to know your river and the effect dam releases have on the water you frequent and it will be highly to your benefit.

Keep a Simple Log With Information Such As:

RIVER CONDITIONS:
Low water
High water
Light stain
Heavy stain
Water temp

WEATHER CONDITIONS:
Windy
Sunny
Overcast
Light showers
Medium showers
Heavy rain

TIME OF DAM RELEASE, CFS AND TIME IT OVER-
TAKES YOUR POSITION:
River conditions after release reached your position

Did the fishing improve or slow down?
Did it rain the night before?  Light, Medium or Heavy

HOW DID THE FISH RESPOND:
Top water action
Just below the surface action
Mid depth action
Near bottom action
Very little action

PLACES STRIKES OCCURRED:
Blowdowns
Close to banks
First drop off
OFFERING USED:
A. Fly or Spinning
      1. Top water
      2. Just below the surface
      3. Near the bottom
            a. Ledges or stone
            b. Points
            c. Edges of current and seams
            d. Near shoals and islands
            e. Shaded areas
            f. Flats or pools
                \*\*\*\*\*\*\*\*\*\*\*\*\*

# The Control System

The most important technique in fly fishing which will enable a person to progress past the beginner stage is the Control System. It amazes me to no end that over half of my fly fishing guests do not use it or are not aware of its importance. The Control System is not something made up by myself or a guides secret but is a simple, etched in stone technique which should be learned by all fly fishermen and women. The Control System is fairly easy to learn and execute. It separates the beginner from the good fishermen.

My clients and I chat frequently throughout our day together. Conversation flows freely. Some clients share their fishing experiences to exotic places. This is always neat to hear about before or during a day on the river. Then, when hooked to a fish the first thing many fly fishermen (or Women) do is reach in front of the rod hand (the hand holding the rod) with their line hand (the hand which retrieves the fly line). They have exposed themselves as beginner fly fishermen even with years of experience. You cannot hide the truth. The hooked fish will usually make a run at them, gain slack and jump off unless we are very lucky.

Sometimes a guest will reach up with their mouth to try and grab line with their lips. The end result most times is the fish escapes. I do not know where this lip technique originated but there are many fly fishermen and women who think it is an acceptable practice. It is not. This is another beginner fisherman to work with or, even sadder, an experienced fisherman who has never progressed past the beginner stage.

How do I help this person advance to another level while not embarrassing them? This presents a positive opportunity for me to advance their expertise in fly fishing by giving a gift which will ensure a higher level of enjoyment of this sport for many years into the future. I tell myself - First and foremost tact must be used. Every fly fishing client is asked if they are familiar with the Control System. Many who have fly fished for a while seemed bored and slightly insulted that I would ask them such a thing. After a lost fish or two they are very inquisitive for positive adjustments which can help.

A frequent gentleman guest of mine is always out

fished by his wife. The husband is a good caster (much better than his wife). He could be a good fisherman if the Control System is brought into play. His wife out fishes him because she can initiate the Control System. She can not cast as far nor does she have quite the fly fishing skills of her husband.

Finally, after mentioning it a half dozen times over the years with a brief description each time, I decided to invest the effort and time until he had it down. I tried not to embarrass him but this action was needed and long overdue in order to aid in his growth as a fly fisherman. (Something very important to both he and his wife). This mistake was constantly hindering them from full enjoyment of their favorite sport. The adjustment we made solved this. It was the only thing preventing him from progressing beyond beginner status to becoming a good fisherman.

(I believe that an expert fly fisherman is a status that is reserved for only a handful of gifted individuals worldwide. It is something I aspire to but will never achieve. To me, the greatest compliment one fisherman can give another is to refer to them as a good fisherman).

Fish kept winning their freedom either on the strike or during the battle, time and time again. His first reaction after the strike is to reach up ahead of the rod hand and grab line - Time and time again. The result being a very high percentage of fish lost.

This is because in each case the fish were able to gain slack and then jump or shake off because of his reaching in front of the rod hand to grab line. It has been a goal of his to land a trophy smallmouth. He has hooked on many occasions fish over four pounds without landing any. My determination to spend almost an hour on this important, line control technique paid off. Two hours later found him landing two nice fish and losing a couple but he finally had the feel of it. The next fish that consumed his Gaines Dynamite, size 4, number 41 color popper was a fat six pound, 22 inch hog. (It was great timing for the largest smallmouth of the season to strike)

One error and she would have escaped. The huge smallie tried to burrow into a sunken tree but he applied just enough pressure, (perfect) turning her at the last moment. Many experienced, diehard smallmouth anglers would drool over a six pound trophy never mind on a fly and on the surface. It was the largest fish caught by a guest during the past 5 seasons.

This same gentleman has an annual smallmouth fishing ritual with a few friends who converge upon a quality bass lake in Maine in early June. They are all decent fly fishermen but not overly advanced. He is their equal in this sport in every regard except for his past lack of using the Control System. Because of this, every outing has been a struggle for him to hold his own with them. Not any longer. Now, I will be able to listen to the stories of the big fish he landed instead of the one that always seemed to get away.

I am amazed that so many fly fishermen who have fished for years still do not know of the simple to execute Control System. Some have fished all over the world with numerous different guides. They tell me the guides have never mentioned the Control System to them. I find this hard to believe. The Control System is very, very important and is used when fly fishing for almost every species. Every good guide knows this. Either the guides did not want to bother teaching the Control System or my guests did not realize its importance and pay attention.

Please allow me to explain how to incorporate the Control System into your fishing. Begin by holding the rod in your rod casting hand and the line between your thumb and index or middle finger of the other hand.

After making the cast, place the line under the index finger and the middle finger of the rod hand. (Fig. 1).

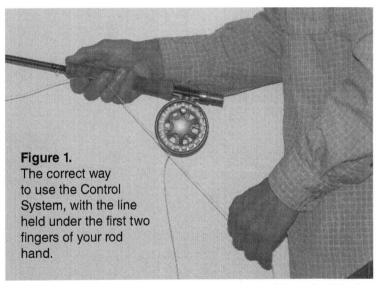

**Figure 1.**
The correct way to use the Control System, with the line held under the first two fingers of your rod hand.

The line is retrieved from below your rod hand with the non-rod hand and across the two fingers (index and middle) of the rod hand. Do not reach above the rod hand to retrieve line after the cast and especially when

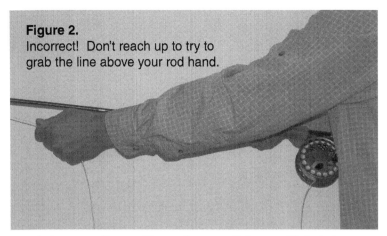

**Figure 2.**
Incorrect! Don't reach up to try to grab the line above your rod hand.

receiving a strike or if you have a fish on. This is important enough to say twice. **Do not reach above the rod hand to retrieve line after the cast** (Fig. 2) and especially when receiving a strike or if you have a fish on. The line is always retrieved from across the two previously mentioned fingers from below the rod hand with the non rod hand. After the cast, go back to the Control System position. Do this over and over again. That is the Control System.

## Using the Control System:

Keep the rod low and pointed towards your fly as it is stripped in or swinging using the Control System. Your goal is for a straight line no slack connection. If the rod is held up a hinge will occur creating slack between the tip and the fly. This will not only prevent good action being presented to the fly because of lack of a straight line connection but may make it difficult to set the hook because of the extra slack provide by the hinge. It also makes you lose contact with the fly, making it difficult to feel a strike.

With the rod pointed low there is a wide distance available to the rod which can be negotiated during a strike. (Greater range of rod movement) This gives a better opportunity for a good hook set and allows you to maintain tension through a larger range of motion with the rod in conjunction with retrieving line through the Control System. The low rod position is more effective in setting the hook, taking up slack line and maintaining tension on the fish. If the rod is held high and a strike occurs, there is only a little distance to move backwards with the rod before slack occurs. A hooked fish will often rush your position creating this slack.

If the rod is low and a strike occurs there is a wide range to move the rod through while quickly stripping in line giving you the benefit of an extra cushion. This is much more effective in setting the hook, omitting slack line and applying a controlled tension on a hooked fish. It is extremely in your favor to be able to maintain a tight line and keep pressure on the fish during this brief, critical period when first receiving a strike and especially true when fishing top water offerings.

When a strike comes use the non rod hand to set the hook by pulling back briskly with the line just as if you were making a long strip. If resistance is felt, immediately set the hook with the rod. Keep the fish under a give and take tension using the Control System - No slack. If the fish wants to run let him go under controlled give and take tension by using the Control System. When they are through running it is your turn to work them back under controlled tension.

Set the hook again after a few seconds. Sometimes you

will feel the weight of the fish and feel that all is well. These bass are fierce battlers. They not only shake their heads but will actually vibrate. That is why a second or third strike is necessary.

Do not keep the rod in a high, straight 12 o'clock position as if fighting a bonefish when playing a small-mouth. This gives them two advantages.

One, it is difficult to gain the proper tension on the line when fishing for smallmouth with a high rod in the straight position. Bring the rod butt closer towards the waist position instead of high overhead. This will more effectively allow the use of the control system in conjunction with quick short strips to eliminate slack and apply tension. Also, a side position of the rod at a 45 degree angle provides more desirable results - less fish lost.

Two, the high rod position, especially a straight high rod allows the smallmouth the tension and best angle for shaking or jumping free. There is little resistance applied to tire them when compared to side 45 degree angle pressure. You are providing the resistance and angle in the straight high rod position which enables the fish to free itself. They shake their heads while vibrating in a furious attempt to shake free from this unknown assailant which has restricted their movement. Danger and panic consume them.

This is a creature which lives in an underwater environment. When pressure is applied in the high rod position the fish is forced with its head up and pulled towards the surface, a place which is away from all it knows as being safe and comfortable.

The high rod position is also the angle which most exactly pulls the offering out of the mouth of the bass, while exerting little actual force compared to 45 degree side pressure. A straight up rod creates the most panic possible from the fish in the first few crucial seconds after hookup. It is these first few seconds which are the most important after the strike. If the fish is brought under control with tension and the proper rod angle in those early moments, the chances for landing the battler is now an advantage for the angler.

Tournament anglers try to keep the fish from coming to the surface and jumping. They do this by keeping their rod near or even below the surface. Too many fish are lost on the jump or at the surface. Remember to maintain constant tension but give line if a run is made. Lower the rod if a jump is made but then immediately get right after them.

In most situations the fish will charge the fisherman. This is where the Control System excels. Quickly retrieve line fast enough to maintain a constant give and take tension below the breaking strength of the tippet. At the strike, most times the fish will immediately rush the angler, making it difficult to take up slack quickly and apply tension. With a lower rod there is a wider arc to work to maintain tension by lifting the rod while also retrieving line Make short, fast, quick strips until you catch up to the fish.

When a fish is on the angler is likely to drop or fumble the line during this crucial moment with longer strips especially immediately after the strike. Longer strips are fine once the fish is under control and you are in the process of casually wearing them down or if adding action while retrieving a cast when trying to solicit a strike. During that moment the fish has struck, the hook is set and an immediate charge towards your position, it is imperative to maintain tension. This is better accomplished with many short, quick strips.

When stripping in the surface fly, keep the rod low and pointed towards the fly so that it reacts to every action of the hand pull. During this time short, medium or long pulls will give a different action to the fly. Find the one which the fish are liking that particular day. Be aware that if you start using too much rod tip when providing action to the fly, slack will develop with each twitch. (I like to analyze every aspect of fly fishing for smallmouth). For every rod twitch used to apply action to a surface offering it will take two strips of line to take up the slack.

If a smallmouth strikes at this time it will take those two strips before you can even start to set the hook with a brisk line pull then another brisk rod movement for the rod set. By using the rod to add action to the fly, you are giving the smallmouth an advantage on the strike. Sometimes it is necessary to add action to the fly with the rod tip but be aware to take up the slack quickly when adding action in this manner.

Retrieve the line when fishing surface offerings by varying the action until favorable results prevail. I like a one – one two with a 1 or 2 second pause to start with.

Switch to a 3 or 4 second pause if results are limited or no pause at all. Start out fairly quickly trying to cover a lot of water but remember, many times it is the pause which is the triggering factor when fishing top waters but not always. Sometimes the bass will hit the fly or plug as it hits the water before action can be added and sometimes they like it faster with smaller or no pauses in between. They may want an 8 – 9 second pause. Experiment. Every day is different.

BRIEF REVIEW: When fly fishing, never reach in front of the hand holding the rod to bring in line at any time after the cast. When hooked up and a fish is charging your position it is imperative that you retrieve with short, quick strips to maintain tension by using the line hand positioned below the hand holding the rod (Control System). Bring in line quickly enough in conjunction with raising the rod to the side to keep constant tension. Short quick strips are the key. Maintain controlled resistance but give line if a run is made. When they are through running it is your turn to apply pressure with the pumping technique allowing no slack. "Never reach in front of the hand holding the rod – Always retrieve line from below the rod hand and especially remember this when hooked to a fish".

*************

# Playing a Fish

An effective technique for playing a fish is called pumping the rod, which is sometimes referred to as the pumping technique. This can be used in either fly fishing or spinning. Maintain a give and take tension as previously mentioned however when you raise the rod do it under tension without reeling in line. Then as you slowly bring the rod down reel in or strip line fast enough to keep slack from occurring. This is the pumping technique. Raise the rod without reeling or stripping in line and then bring in line as you lower it. This is done under a give and take tension or set reel drag without allowing slack to develop. Keep constantly under tension without allowing slack. Lift the rod up from 9:30 to the 11 o'clock position without bringing in line (reeling or stripping) then go back down to 9:30 while taking up line just enough to keep tension allowing no slack at any time. Keep a 45 degree angle when possible.

Do not raise your rod high overhead when floating in a boat. You are already at a raised distance above the waters surface depending on the craft. If wading and a hooked fish makes a run towards rocky terrain then it may be necessary to lift the rod overhead at a 45 degree angle.

Keep the butt of the rod in the area of your waistline when fighting a fish. You have better control and are in position to make adjustments much quicker with less chance for error.

As the fish begins to come closer to the boat continue to keep the rod position to more of a side angle instead of straight up and down. This, in conjunction with pumping the rod will help to land the fish a little quicker. The longer the fish is on the better chance to escape. Playing the fish correctly translates to a better chance of survival, when released.

In smallmouth fishing getting the fish on the reel is optional. If you do choose to play a fish from the reel be careful. An involuntary action that usually goes unnoticed is the brisk shaking of the rod and tip when line is wound onto the reel. The movement occurring at the area of the reel and grip is compounded by the time it reaches the rod tip. A nice fish can be easily shaken off. Be aware that most smallmouth hooked will immediately rush your position. It is imperative that line be taken up quickly at this moment. That is why many experienced fly fishing anglers will concentrate on quickly using the Control System to take up line and maintain tension instead of trying to get them on the reel. Most fish are lost when trying to get them on the reel at this critical moment while fly fishing for smallmouth bass or trout.

BRIEF REVIEW : Make sure a fish is under control before attempting to get them on the reel or else play them exclusively without using the reel and its drag. When trying to place the fish onto the reel do it smoothly without jerky motions of the rod or tip. (Be aware of this during your next hookup and you will notice exactly what I am referring to).

Work the fish back while not allowing slack to develop (even briefly) but do have the drag adjusted well below breaking strength of the line (if the reel is used) so as to give line during a run by the fish. Do this until ready to land. Don't rush it. I would much rather lose a fish because it became unbuttoned knowing that everything was done correctly than to make a mistake and lose the fish. Many green fish (green fish are those which still have plenty of fight left) are lost that could have become a fond memory because of a half hearted stab or two of the net or a premature attempt to land. You will find that each run will become shorter with less electricity as the fish tires. It is just a matter of time now. Be patient and enjoy the battle until with control and composure you are ready to land and release the prize.

*************

# Effectiveness of Fly Fishing the Surface

There is no other method as effective for enticing top water strikes by smallmouth bass as fly fishing the surface with a floating line.

There are top water fly imitations available along with rod and line manipulations which can offer realistic impressions of prey along with efficiency unobtainable with spinning gear. You do not need to bring the fly all the way in before recasting as in spinning. Just work the promising area, (usually less than one quarter of the cast) make one back cast and hit a new productive target. (When fly fishing sub surface work the offering all the way back to the boat). There is triple the effective coverage in the same amount of time when fly fishing the surface.

This enables you to present a fly to more targets effectively and effortlessly. It is possible to cast with a surface fly so efficiently that it seems like the targets are surgically dissected. The more targets your fly can be presented to with the less time spent in unproductive water will equal more strikes during an outing. Fly fishing the surface excels at this.

We have experienced active fish holding on the narrow downstream section of a large sunken tree, especially when there is a depth transition provided by a current velocity build up caused by the thicker part above and gouging out a washout below. This is a great holding position for a feeding smallmouth to take advantage of prey which has been overcome and brought through by the current. Do not give up after casting to all the best looking areas of a downed tree. Make sure to stay with it and fish the downstream side. I hook just as many fish from this secondary target as the prime areas.

A high percentage of strikes when top water fly fishing become solid hookups. Imperative in both fly fishing and spinning is a proper hookset, keeping hooks sharp and maintaining tension on the fish. Barbless, sharp hooks will enable better penetration at the strike but it is imperative that no slack be given or the fish will easily escape. I prefer sharp, barbless hooks for all guests because the fish are usually well hooked a higher percentage of the time. With a little coaching my guests are able to maintain the necessary tension on the line. There are very few days throughout the season that enough smallmouth to make a days fishing interesting cannot be coaxed to strike at the surface providing the river is in not heavily stained from rain or a large dam release, running extremely low and warm, or an approaching front with a brisk wind is coming in.

Some anglers would rather receive a few visible strikes on the surface than several below. Anglers preferences come into play when the fish are reluctant to accept surface fare.

It is important to be ready every second your offering is on the water. Try to concentrate. It seems like the fish wait for you either look away or not be paying attention even for a split second. You can have great concentration all day while on the water but advert your attention for a second or two and that is when the strike of the day will occur. I do not know why this is but it has happened to my guests on too many occasions. Why is it always the largest fish in the river that do this?

Observation is very important especially on those challenging days. Be ready for any clues the river may share. Look for the little dimple or boil. Hear the sound of a feeding fish then quickly respond. Pay attention to concentrations of insects. The fish are. Look at the river conditions of the moment tuning into where the best places for a smallmouth to hold are. Trust your intuition.

The strike from a smallmouth is much different than hanging up on the bottom. It has the feel of a living thing usually not the same as a momentary snag. If you think a strike occurred there is a very good chance it did.  When fishing the surface and the top water offering is stuck to a tree or piece of vegetation a foot or two below the surface you received a strike.

Fly fishing top waters requires quickly gaining control of the line after casting.  Sometimes, even a second before the fly or lure hits the water a bass will explode upon it.  This is a helpless situation.  There is little that can be done.  Before a strike can be initiated the fish will be gone.

Another benefit of making a straight line pull when fly fishing the surface is, if the strike is missed (no hookup) the fly will still be in the strike zone.  This is one of the magic moments in fly fishing for smallmouth.

It can weigh heavily on the nerves while wondering if the bass has moved on or is viewing your offering while pondering another go at it.

Let the fly or top water plug sit there for 5 to ten seconds before giving it a couple of twitches.  Then allow it to remain motionless for another 5 - 10 seconds before repeating.  Move on after two or three casts.

Another technique is to recast to the same area three times moving the fly or lure through as quickly as possible, even too quick for a reaction by the fish.  Then on the fourth cast work it back very slowly leaving 5 - 10 seconds between subtle twitches.  It is exciting when a big smallmouth plays this cat and mouse game with you before finally striking.  Many a fine memory has been earned in this manner.

Try to make the cast toward the downstream area on an approximate forty-five degree angle as the boat floats along. This helps to give a better drift when fishing the surface (fly or spinning) or when casting nymphs with or without a strike indicator. Our goal when using surface flies (or spinning top waters) is to hit the target and then give the offering a twitch or two without moving it more than a couple of inches. Then give another twitch with a slight pause while still only moving the fly or plug slightly. Repeat this several times before recasting. We may receive a quick strike as the fly or plug barely lands on the water, but most times it is the pause after the twitch which is the triggering factor.

Another important reason for casting to the downstream side as the boat casually drifts along is that it will allow you to keep the fly or spinning plug in the productive zone longer while it is twitched and paused. This is imperative. A cast slightly behind the boat will pull the offering out of the productive zone too quickly, usually before it has a chance to solicit a strike from a willing participant. When the fisherman in the front casts straight to the bank or slightly back upriver as the boat floats along, he or she will interfere with the fishing of the angler in the back of the boat. In this scenario, the front angler will constantly and ineffectively fish the rear angler's water. This translates to less action for each.

*************

# Techniques

Smallmouth are more opportunistic than trout so usually a few fly or lure patterns will offer success. On many days an offering which brings strikes in early afternoon will not towards evening or a fly that had worked earlier that morning may not interest fish towards late morning or early afternoon.

It is important to change up when receiving a lack of interest for an extended period over water known to hold fish. If not receiving action, be ready to move attention from the bank and concentrate on the first or second drop off from the bank, where there is a change of depth. One technique with a sub surface sink tip is to cast toward the shoreline, make 8 to 10 strips then cast again, or cast to the first drop , make 8 to 10 strips then cast again.

A good technique is to anchor or slow the craft down by rowing while keeping a fixed position above a targeted area. Allow a fly to swing through the perceived productive water while mending for a deeper running of your fly through this area. Use this technique during a days fishing by reading the water to pinpoint good fish holding structure. Allow the fly to swing through as many of these identified areas as possible. The productive water should be downstream of your position with this method.

Try a mend or two to start, then allow the fly to pass through the productive area adding another mend or two to soften the abruptness of the swing. Wait an extra few seconds. Most times it feels like the cast is over but the fly is really still swinging and at its most effective position for receiving a strike. If no strikes try more mends to gain depth while the fly passes through runs, pockets, heads and tails of pools. (A run is located below a rapid or riffle where a noticeable depth change occurs. Runs usually hold fish.)

Sometimes I will anchor above these areas allowing my guests to swing flies using sink tips or lures though them. When finished working these runs, the anchor is pulled then redropped 10 to 15 feet downstream to repeat while covering the entire run, swinging our flies, lures or plugs to the waiting trout or smallmouth. (Anchoring in this manner is not recommended for canoes or kayaks except in slow or non current areas).

Position above the target then cast straight across or slightly downstream, add a few mends then allow the velocity of the current to present and swing the fly. Add additional mends if needed for additional depth. Follow your line with the rod tip and try to stay in touch with the fly. This technique works for fly fishing or spinning, wading or fishing from a boat.

The day begins by rigging two or three rods (fly or spin) two for the surface and a third for subsurface work. If surface action is stingy we set up an additional sub surface rod and then work that area. The same can be accomplished with one rod by changing lures or flies. It is not quite as efficient but will work much better than presenting one offering all day.

About every thirty minutes try a top water offering to see if the smallies have changed their preference. If success is limited near the bank try working the first drop off from the bank with the top water offering. If little or no success go below the surface.

A huge benefit of being on the water nearly every day allows use of the info gained from previous recent outings. The conditions change from day to day. The smallmouth are forced to adapt as it does. It could be a change in the weather, an approaching low pressure system or a heavy rain the day before stained the water.

Consistency in fish feeding activity will usually prevail if the weather and river conditions remain the same without brisk wind or heavy staining of the water. A sustained wind may be evident, the sun may be high or it may be cloudy, lack of rain or on the other side of the coin a dam release may give too much water or not enough. Any of these and many other variables can affect the feeding mode of our target species. Sometimes it can be for the better and sometimes more challenging.

Break the river into four different levels. The first is the surface or near the surface, the next is one to three feet down followed by three to six feet down and the last 6 to 10 feet. Very seldom will you need to concentrate below the 8 - 10 foot depth on most rivers.

When fly fishing, all these depths can be effectively reached with 3 separate type of lines – the floater can be used with surface flies or bead heads and cone heads for different levels of subsurface work. Non-weighted streamers can be used with a floater for fishing on or just below the surface.

Decrease the size of the tippet when going subsurface with a floating line. A switch to subsurface with the same line will need a 4 to 6 pound tippet added to afford a more desirable drop and action and less of a chance for fish detecting a fraud.

My preference and the preference of almost all my guests is for the surface. Top water strikes from smallmouth can be addicting. Sometimes they are not willing to take on the surface. This is usually when we will place our attention below but will remain perceptive throughout the day for surface opportunities especially during the last few hours of daylight.

Some guests would rather remain fishing the surface

even though the action is limited because they enjoy the ferocity of a surface strike so much that they would rather catch fewer fish but be able to see the strike.

As you will conclude, when the sun starts losing its full impact upon the water usually beginning between four and five pm a top water bite may develop. This occurs nearly every day from late spring through early fall. The first few hours after sunrise can also offer good top water action. When a dam release reaches our position feeding activity can increase and a surface bite can begin.

It is pretty much the same for spinning except we are using a different method but still presenting our offerings in the same places. When using either method begin the day by casting towards the bank with a top water, unless previous outings suggest the fish may be receptive near the first or second drop off, flats, pools, ledges, sunken trees, etc. The quiet edges of gravel bars, shoals and islands, (mentioned earlier) are other good targets for top waters or sub surface especially where a depth change or current seam occurs. If limited success is achieved on the surface go deeper unless there exists a preference for the surface.

When going below, first cover the area a foot or two below the surface then two to four feet and then deeper. A floating, number 7 or 9 Rapala can effectively fish the surface to 3 feet below. Use 4 pound test line with a quick retrieve to allow this plug to gain more depth. Work the same plug very slowly with slight occasional twitches and it will stay on or near the surface. Use a steady slow retrieve for 1 foot below. With this same plug the surface, one, two and three foot below can be covered while using a different retrieve and a lighter line.

Offerings can be fished slower or quicker with or without weight to give a slightly different look to the fish and also cover different depths.

Be creative. If the surface offers little success when spinning and the fish are not responding to a Rapala or Rapala type baits try Fluke-style soft plastics before going to deeper diving Rapalas or crankbaits, tubes, jigs or worms both Senko style and curly tail. By using this concept large areas of water and different depths can be prospected in a short amount of time.

Basically, we are trying to pattern the fish. A pattern is the type of offering, depth and structure most of the fish are willing to feed at or on during that particular time. Sometimes it will be certain structure such as stone or wood. They may be receptive towards the bank, blow downs, shade or the first drop off. The hot spot could be where depth occurs near gravel bars, islands, flats, pools or set backs or on the edges of faster water or current lanes.

Be aware that there is a prime spot above a river obstruction in fast water such as a boulder, ledge or a downed tree and not just below. This is because a cushion of slower holding water exists on the upstream side of any object in current as well as the obvious break the obstruction itself provides downstream.

In essence, try to concentrate on where the fish are

most likely to be, and what they are most likely to be feeding on. The more variables you can quickly eliminate lets you narrow the possibilities and focus on what the fish may be willing to accept at that particular moment.

Spinner baits are another alternative when spinning in one quarter to three eights ounce sizes using a Colorado, Indiana (deeper cupped) or Willow Leaf blade or blades. Combinations of different blades are used with good success. Spinner Baits are a good option in windy conditions, especially towards the bank. The bait fish are pushed up against the wind blown banks and the smallmouth will be there. Good basic colors for the spinnerbait skirt are white, yellow, chartreuse and a similar color of the natural forage of baitfish available.

If still no success it may be time to go deeper or concentrate on the drop off from the bank. Sometimes they will be on the current lane out from the bank usually near the first or second drop off.

Soft plastics such as tubes (3 - 5 inch), worms (3 - 7 inch) or jigs (3 - 5 inch) are good alternatives for near the bottom presentations. Use 1/16, 1/8 or 3/16 ounce environmentally friendly weight for tube fishing. For Senkos – Use weightless, texas rigged, wacky style or drop shot.

Do not overlook curly tail grubs in the 3 – 5 inch range. Also the same size swim baits. Berkeley rigged power minnows and swim baits and Storm rigged curly tail and swim baits catch lots of fish every season wherever they are used. They are effective and inexpensive with different weight heads running from 1/16 oz. to 1/8 or 3/16 oz. weight, the choice of which depends upon conditions.

Use the lightest head possible which will get the job done. (That allows the offering to drop in a way which has a desirable presentation and spends as much time as possible in the strike zone).

Cast to targets instead of fishing all the water blindly. Allow a sub surface lure, plug or fly to swing through these targets such as in front of, below and parallel to downed tree, large rock or boulder. Allow the current (if available) to work the lure for you.

Target pockets, slicks, the edge of dark water (depth change), shaded areas, drop offs, cuts in the bank, runs ( a run is downstream of a riffle or rapid where a change in depth occurs), edges of fast water, entering tributaries, gravel bars and the upstream and downstream side of islands.

Depth and control will be best achieved by raising or lowering the rod as the offering is steered through good fish holding structure. Reel in just fast enough to keep the spinning blades turning, spoon wobbling or good plug action continuing.

Concentrate on the drift in both fly fishing and spinning but more importantly on the swing. Plan for the swing to occur through or in the area of a perceived productive target. Most strikes occur through or at the end of this swing. That is when your offering will begin to rise from the bottom due to the increased velocity influence at this point by the current.

This causes the blades, spoon, plug or fly to give off more vibration and fish attracting action. Do not be over anxious in starting another cast. Make sure the swing is complete, then wait a few more seconds. Try to capitalize on this productive part of the cast by spending those extra few seconds right in there.

Sometimes if spinning, it can help to flip the bail at the end of the swing and just before retrieving. Allow line to feed out and then engage. The current will reactivate the offering when the line again tightens giving another fish-catching opportunity several feet downstream from where the last cast and swing ended. There has been many outings this technique has produced a few extra fish for my guests. Be ready.

When hooked up to a fish in current try to get the boat to the slower water near the shoreline. I see more fish lost (both smallmouth and trout) from inexperienced boaters because they try to fight and land the fish while maintaining position in the faster water. I have also seen guests play and lose fish from a drift boat with other guides because the guide did not slide the boat out of the faster water. The first thing we need to do is to take away the advantage the fish has thanks to the current. This allows us to fight just the fish without the additional velocity of the whole river. The fish does not need to work as hard but still applies a very heavy resistance as if three times its size and this in only a moderate current.

If by yourself and hooked up with a nice fish in faster water, allow the boat to drift with the flow. Be aware of the boats path (for obvious safety reasons) while playing the fish. Try to bring the craft into the quiet shoreline water if an opportunity presents itself and then pressure the fish away from the fast water. A hooked fish will not be able to use the force of the current to its advantage if the boat is not in a fixed position.

Be aware that when floating a river, for the most part, you will be drifting with the current. Do not make too many casts to a good looking section of water at the expense of missing other targets. River floating is about making as many good casts as possible to different targets while attempting to initiate a positive response from a fish. In set backs and very slow current areas it is more practical to work the water but in steady current areas with slower bank water you will be better served by not over casting to one target at the expense of missing other opportunities.

BUSTING BAIT
This is one of the exciting moments when pursuing smallmouth bass. First there will be bait fish breaking the surface in an erratic fashion. They may be followed by one or more aggressive smallmouth working for a meal.

Sometimes there will be violent splashing of the larger attacking bass and sometimes there will be visible, moving wakes with the bait fish jumping ahead. You may just see baitfish jumping themselves. They are not doing this for exercise.

Immediately present your offering into the fray as quickly as possible. There is a short window so do not hesitate. Strikes in this scenario almost always result in solid hookups. Cast whatever fly, plug, lure or soft bait is the most available for a quick reaction on your part – Top water or sub surface. My interpretation is, its all good.

If a fish or group of fish are successful in the pursuit they are in a delighted state. Because of their makeup the only thing that could make them even happier at this moment is another surefire feeding opportunity. However, if the group came up empty or even a single fish came up empty, they will be frantic to strike at almost anything.

The group of smallmouth will feel the frustration of their still hungry companion and will be just as frantic to pursue and devoir a helpless prey item. You will encounter no surer high percentage shot at receiving a vicious strike than bass busting bait. Remember, the window is short, with every second beyond a few a decrease in the opportunity.

************

# Improving Fly Fishing Skills

Many folks have difficulty getting started in fly fishing. Acquiring equipment, learning the basics and still being headed in the right direction can be quite challenging. It seems to be an even greater challenge to improve fly fishing and fly casting skills beyond a certain point.

Most of us reach a level or plateau quickly, usually the first season or two and then bottom out. It is difficult to improve skills in fly fishing beyond an existing, invisible barrier. This will be the focus of the following suggestions. For me, luck as it applies to fishing is defined as when preparation and opportunity come together.

Lets get started...

## Spend Time with Experienced Fishermen:
Joining a club or organization (Such as Trout Unlimited) can help to accomplish this especially if you do not have experienced fishing friends who are willing to share information. Consider joining a fly tying class. Most meet one night a week for a four to six week period for a very modest cost. Not only will experienced fishermen be there but during these fly tying classes there will be a lot more discussed than just tying flies. Fishing stories are shared, tips on fly casting are given, techniques under diverse conditions for sought after species in wonderful places are spoken about, favorite fishing spots are given up and quite often an invitation to fish may be offered. Fishing contacts are made and the top recommended guides will be referred to. Demonstrating the highest values will often help to convince these folks to share valuable knowledge. Become involved while giving some of your time and energy.

## Consider Hiring a Guide
for the type of fishing you are interested in. Make sure to tell him or her that although catching fish would be nice, more importantly learning as much as possible under actual fishing conditions is the main goal. Most guides are on the water 100 to 150+ days every season and under pressure to produce during most endeavors. They possess a wealth of knowledge gained through years of dedication to the type or types of fishing they engage in. A good guide can save many years of floundering and get you on track after an outing or two.

Some may also share with you their favorite fishing place or places.

## I Suggest to Get Started by Purchasing a Beginner or Middle of the Road Outfit

consisting of a rod, reel, line, vest and waders. The other incidentals such as forceps, fly assortment, fly boxes, leaders, nippers, sunglasses, scissor pliers, sunglasses, etc. can be purchased just before you are ready to hit the water. Each company's fly rod has a slightly different feel which sets them apart. Because of this you should audition at least a few before purchasing one. A good way to proceed is purchase a starter outfit from a reputable company which stands behind their products. An upgrade can be made later if desired when more familiar with equipment and preferences.

## Learn to Read a Stream

Learn about the dead drift & cross stream swing concept. Focus this dead drift and cross stream swing through good fish holding structure. When executing the swing give it time to complete itself. Many folks will pick up to make another cast when the swing is in its finest position for soliciting a strike. Manipulate the line or rod with slight twitches or pulls during or at the end of the swing to help bring an extra strike or two. Be in control of and in touch with your offering at all times.

## Try Methods Other Than Just the Surface

For years I convinced myself to just fish surface flies by saying that I was a dry fly man. In reality, I did not want to take the time or apply the effort to learn how to fish nymphs or streamers. I did not have confidence when fishing below the surface. Since learning, thousands of beautiful trout and smallmouth bass have been deceived by my guests or myself using methods other than dry. Now, please do not misunderstand. A surface preference is still sought however if the fish are not willing on top, we use other methods while remaining constantly alert and perceptive for surface opportunities.

## Become a Better Caster

Start out by limiting your practice sessions to no more than 1/2 hour at a time for three to five days a week. Any practice session more than a half hour does more harm than good. A good time to start practicing is 4 – 6 weeks before the actual fishing season begins. For myself, once guiding starts there is little time to practice so I need to have my casting fine tuned before each season starts. On some trips I may ask a person to cast into a certain area and then make a request that they give their line a few mends or manipulations. Some may ask me to physically show them how. That is why I need to have the ability to pick a rod up in the middle of the day and make one cast and have it drop perfectly.

If you have a good size lawn that will do, otherwise go to a park or grassy mowed area where there is no chance of striking anyone with the fly line. Use the Control System discussed in detail in its own chapter.

Start by casting just the line you can handle well with good tight loops. Lengthen until form and control is difficult to maintain. This is the point you should not go beyond until form and control is mastered at this distance. The way to accomplish this is to shorten up then cast with good form. Slowly lengthen the cast until you once again come to the point where good form is hard to control. Stop, then repeat.

The important aspect of this method of improving fly casting is to always work within the area your able to control with good tight loops and good form. Then slowly lengthen until it becomes difficult to control and then stop and start over. It is more important to cast under control than to make longer sloppy casts. Remember, you are not going to the races or trying to impress anyone. You are trying to improve your fly casting.

Take your time, relax, loosen the shoulders and try to develop good control with nice tight loops. It is very important to finish each session casting with good form, even if a short 20 to 30 foot cast is it.

Do not be concerned about distance at this time. Casting distance along with the amount of line you are able to hold in the air under control will begin increasing in two or three weeks or less. This will take a half hour session (no more) four to five days a week. The key is to take your time and try to maintain form while slowly lengthening the cast until once again it becomes sloppy. Stop, then repeat.

Remember to stop the rod at 11 o'clock and then the 1 o'clock position, with an abrupt stop at each. It may help to visualize during the power snap portion of the cast that you are:

1. Throwing an apple from a stick for distance.

2. Snapping a towel in a gym locker room.

3. Practicing a karate chop. An abrupt speed up and stop should occur in the approximate 11 o'clock position on the forward cast and the 1 o'clock position on the back cast. Make the back cast at a 45 to 65 degree angle to the side and the forward cast at a 90 degree angle straight over the shoulder.

The benefits of this technique and casting style is to help develop a better casting rhythm and there is also less chance of the line running into itself. It is traveling in two separate planes, instead of forward and back over the shoulder. This is a style which is also much more forgiving of slight casting errors, which occur on occasion for all of us.

The shorter & quicker the speed up and stop motion (similar to the snapping towel, throwing of an apple from a stick, or a karate chop) the tighter and more efficient the loop occurring in the forward or back cast. This means you are using good form and will be able to cast further with less effort because of less wind resistance with the tighter more aerodynamic loops. When a snapping noise occurs, you are not waiting long enough between the forward and back cast. Wait another half second and that should alleviate the snapping noise.

Picture yourself driving on the highway at 65 miles an hour with groceries on the back seat. All of a sudden someone drives their car in front of you. When you hit the brakes what will happen to the groceries sitting on the back seat? Chances are they will propel forward onto the front seat or the window. This is because the energy which was created had an outlet to release when you stepped on the brakes. Basically, it was speed, then an abrupt stop. That is what you are trying to accomplish when fly casting with an abrupt speed up and stop motion. The difference is you are attempting to execute under a controlled situation while achieving a desired result.

When casting split shot, heavier weighted flies or heavier sink tips or sinking lines open up your casting stroke to a 10 to 2 or even 9:30 to 2:30 position with less of a snap at each position. A smoother slower motion is desired. You cannot reasonably cast split shot or heavier weighted flies and still maintain tight, crisp loops. Your leader will tangle. Also when using a strike indicator with shot a more open stroke is needed. The areas many fly casters need to make adjustments are:

A. Pushing the cast between 1 and 11 with the absence of a speed up and stop (power snap). Because many fly fishermen or fly fisherwoman begin with a spinning background, they tend to revert back to the spinning forward motion when fly casting. This is especially true with gentlemen having a great deal of strength. All their lives they have been able to compensate with effort and strength. This will not produce desired results in fly fishing. It is technique and timing that win the day not strength.

I have on many occasions had guests who were only able to cast 10 feet. After working with them for a few minutes they were able to triple that. If someone desires to improve fly casting skills it will be necessary to spend a little time practicing until the feel is developed (timing and technique).

B. Not making an abrupt stop at 11 (forward cast) or 1 (back cast).

C. Snapping noise. Usually means you are not waiting long enough between the forward or back cast. Try waiting another half second.

D. Bringing the rod too far back or too far forward towards the 9 or 3 position. Use 11 and 1 as a guide. For shot, heavy weighted flies, sinking lines or indicator fishing a 10 to 2 or 9 to 3 position is desired.

E. Finishing the forward cast in the 7 to 9 direction. This usually causes the generated line speed and cast to crash in a downward direction. Your line will follow the direction of the rod tip. If you finish the final casting stroke headed downward the cast will finish in the same direction.

F. Executing the forward power snap higher than the rear back cast will create tailing loops and tangles.

G. Not lowering the rod and taking up all slack before beginning the back cast with the rod tip pointed at the fly. This will allow you to maintain control and have a direct influence over the fly line from the moment the back cast begins. Beginner to intermediate fly fishermen or woman will usually begin their backcast with a high rod and a huge slack hinge of fly line. They are destined for a poor cast from the start. A straight line connection with the rod pointing down and towards the fly line with slight tension before beginning the back cast is desired.

H. Breaking the wrist – The wrist should be an extension of the forearm. They should become one. It may help to place the end of the rod in your sleeve or tape the rod to your wrist to help develop the feel. Also consider the purchase of a wrist lock made specifically for beginners to intermediate fly fisher persons trying to learn or improve their fly casting. It is important to minimize the breaking of the wrist and use the wrist and forearm together as one, during the casting stroke for both the forward and back cast.

I. Not slightly lowering the rod tip after the finishing forward cast nears completion. You do not need an exaggerated motion. What is needed is a slight lowering of the rod after the final forward cast which enables the fly line to not be pulled backwards by the high rod tip.

J. Compensating with poor casting by over powering the cast. It is technique and timing that is desired, not strength. The harder you work with poor casting technique and timing the least distance the line and fly will travel. It is very frustrating. Take your time, cast 11 to 1 with a short speed up and stop at each, relax and do not practice longer than a half hour. The motion between the speed up and stop is easy and relaxed. Concentrate on good form and small tight loops instead of distance. The quicker and sharper the speed up and stop at 1 and 11 the tighter the loops. Distance will come. Make sure each session is ended with controlled casting and nice tight loops even if the distance is short. Eventually more and more line can be slowly added by using a controlled cast. This means you will be able to decently hold a lot of line in the air and be pleased with your form. That is the true measure - Personal approval or disapproval of your own casting performance.

K. Working more line than can be controlled. Many times a snapping noise will be evident. (Moving ahead or back a little too soon) Try casting the line which can be controlled and shoot the difference until more practice is possible. More practice will enable the holding of more line in the air between forward and back casts under control. Always be in control of the line you are able to cast.

L. Estimate the amount of line you will need to cast and try to have most of it already stripped from the reel and ready to go. This is a pet peeve of many guides. One situation which comes to mind is when a trout or smallmouth has shown itself by feeding on an insect or chasing bait on or near the surface. Usually the cast needs to be made quickly to achieve the best results (An acceptance by the fish). When a guest makes a short strip and a false cast and then another and another and then another and then another and another and another when our quarry is out there begging for the fly, the guide will usually just shake their head and cry (within). Then, a good guide will show the guest how to correctly prepare for the next feeding smallmouth or trout.

Strip the line necessary to accomplish the cast quickly off the reel, make a couple of false casts then shoot the rest. This method is much quicker in reaching a feeding fish and there is less chance of alerting the trout with all that false casting. Make sure the fly line itself does not pass over or too close to the trout's position where its movement or shadow may spook the fish.

## Learn to identify Insect Rise Forms:

Rise forms usually will offer clues to what the fish are feeding on and what stage of development. The better insect books have good information which will help. Rise forms give clues as to what stage of what insect is probably causing a fish to make that particular rise form and what to use as an offering. This is usually something very important when trout fishing for selective fish. Smallmouth are much less fussy and will accept most flies or top water offerings when feeding on or near the surface even if off size or color from what they are actually feeding upon at the moment. Still, it is challenging fun and exciting to cast small size 18 or 20 flies to the bronze battlers when they are feeding on them.

Learn at least a little about the entomology (the study of insects) of the waters you fish. This will help decision making regarding the fly choice by giving an understanding of the insect be it surface, in the film or sub surface. It will also give a leg up if a large trout is encountered while smallmouth fishing or you find yourself on a trout pond or stream.

## The Predator/Prey Concept - Make it Work for You.

The Predator/Prey Concept is the way a predator relates to its prey. Think of a barn cat and a mouse or a lion stalking an antelope. They each do not rush their perceived meal because in most cases it will escape.

First they observe and then formulate a plan. Next they stalk slowly and quietly while maintaining a low silhouette. All during this time their concentration is at its peak while with as little commotion as possible, they shorten the distance. This is the Predator/Prey Concept.

We may not need to go through such extremes but be aware of trying to not make the fish aware of your presence. Do not just rush in and start fishing. Take a little time to analyze the situation and develop a plan. If things are not going your way when casting to a fish, step back, review and then make the necessary adjustments.

I can remember one fine early morning while scouting a small stream with my wife. We pulled up alongside a heavily shaded, pretty stream located on a lightly traveled gravel road in Voluntown, Connecticut. I was ready first and decided to take a quick look at the pool about 60 feet down the bank. There were three 14 – 15 inch brown trout lazily feeding on spent tricos. What a pretty sight. I whispered to Susan what I saw. In her haste to join me she shut the car door a little too briskly. I could barely hear it from my position but more importantly the trout felt the vibration.

Two of them immediately spooked and the other casually followed suit. My wife asked where the trout were when she arrived. I explained to her what had happened. This experience made me aware of how important the Predator/Prey Concept is. It also made me wonder about how many times a person ruined their own opportunity for successful fishing and never knew it.  How many times have I been guilty of this?

## Watch Fishing DVDs

These offer what I refer to as the most information bang for the buck and take the least investment of time.  They cover nearly all aspects of fishing.  Watch the ones of interest to you at least a couple of times each. Take notes and use them as a point of reference.  Review every pre season and perhaps reference them during the season.

## Read Books and Magazines

Use them as future reference points.  Many magazines contain key excerpts from informative books.  There is also a vast amount of specific fishing information on the internet depending on your interest.

## Tie Good Knots

I have been fly fishing for over 30 years and in that time have lost more than one nice fish because of a poor knot.  The most vivid experience which comes to mind happened a few years ago in Upstate New York while pursuing Steelhead on the Salmon River.  It was the end of November.  The fishing was slow because of the cold front which seemed to shut the bite down.  The temps were in the low to mid twenties with wind.  After two and a half days of hard fishing I had one bite and missed the set.  One hour before it was time to leave for home I received a quick & hard strike.  The steelhead made a short run and leaped from the water.  A beautiful male with bright red cheeks and a double iridescent stripe running down its side.  An incredible specimen - at least 14 or 15 pounds.

The fish held in mid air and time stood still for that

magic second or two. The next run and leap was more of the same and then another. All of a sudden contact was lost. I quickly stripped in line as fast as possible believing this trophy had rushed my position and created slack. It has happened to me before. When the end of my leader was inspected, there for the whole world to see was a curly cue where a size 10 Green Butt Skunk should be. This is a sure sign that a poor knot was tied and slipped.

Man, what a disappointment. My thoughts drifted to a few moments before. In a hurry to tie the last knot, I did not take the time to cinch it down properly. "Good enough," I remember telling myself. Three days of tough conditions had taken its toll. This fish would have been so satisfying. I hung in there and did everything right until the last cast but it wasn't meant to be. The reason it wasn't meant to be was I had a momentary lapse in concentration and did not tie a good knot. All the good things I had done with excellent concentration during the previous three days meant nothing. When it really counted I had succumbed to broken concentration.

When should you tie a good knot? Every single knot tied should be a good knot. You just never know when the fish of the day, the fish of the season or the fish of a lifetime is going to strike. Be ready with a good knot.

## Hook Sets and Playing a Fish

There are many variables which depend on conditions, equipment used and species pursued. A different hook set and equipment will be needed for a bass in heavy cover compared to a trout sipping midges on a quiet flat or a  steelhead in heavy pocket water or a king salmon who has just moved up from a rapid into a large tailout.

Usually the correction needed will be for too hard a hook set, too light, too fast, too slow or low and downstream instead of high and straight back. A gentle lifting of the rod or a quick wrist movement is necessary, especially when fishing nymphs for trout. For steelhead, salmon or even smallmouth a hook set low and in the downstream direction usually will result in more solid hookups. Sometimes this will hold true for stream and river trout as well. Experience and good concentration will enable the development of perception for good hook sets. In the meantime try not to yank the fish behind you into the trees. Remember to use the (previously mentioned) control system.

## Playing a Fish

There are many variables depending on conditions, equipment used and the species being pursued. I like to use the pumping technique. Basically, when the fish wants to run you let him go. Try to maintain a 45 degree angle to the fish. When they are thru running its your turn to work. Keep the rod 45 degrees to the side while keeping the line taunt with no slack. Only reel or bring in line as the rod is brought downward while smoothly pumping the rod up without reeling.

Give them side pressure during the fight , especially when getting them closer. This will help to confuse and tire the fish quickly. Pressure them down and dirty if headed towards an underwater obstruction. Do the same if the fish gets into current. Be patient and try to do everything right and be in control of composure. I would much rather lose a fish because they just came unbuttoned rather than lose one because of a mistake. Play them until they are ready, then do the deed. Use the Control System allowing no slack while giving and taking line.

If it is a larger fish get them on the reel but only after they are under control. Otherwise play them from the line itself. Do not reach up with your mouth and try to take up loose line caused by a hot charging fish. Usually the fish will win their freedom leaving you a frustrated fisherman with a mouth full of fly line. Try to keep the line taunt at all times.

Wet your hands before handling and releasing a fish. Limit the handling and release the fish as soon as possible, when properly revived. I like to feel life coming back into the fish just before it swims away under its own power.

## Observation and Concentration

All skills and information learned will be of little value without good observation & concentration. They are the final barrier which will help bridge the gap in order to become a good fly fisherman. Good observation and concentration will enable you to best utilize all information and experience, when, where and how by blending them together on a split second's notice with hand and eye coordination. They will help you detect and adapt to subtle messages and perceptions.

Last but not least, they help you to do all the little things consistently correct during the course of an outing. A good fish seems to always strike at an inopportune time. You can be fishing for 8 hours and 59 minutes with great concentration, but if you do not pay attention for a few seconds that is when the fish of the day will strike. I do not know why this happens so often but it does and enough for me to be concerned. When your offering is in the water pay attention.

************

# Putting It All In Perspective

By now many of you may feel there is just too much information to learn for this fly fishing to be fun. Remember that fly fishing is a relative sport. You can purchase inexpensive equipment and a few flies and go out and have many great experiences. You could make fly fishing your life long passion, spend thousands upon thousands dollars and have a wonderful time of it. The sport of fly fishing can be enjoyed any place in between.

Please allow me to share a story which may put this all into perspective. A long time ago there was a king who wanted to possess the entire fly fishing knowledge in the world. He called his wise men before him, told them of his wishes and sent them to the four corners of the earth to gather this information.

Five years later they returned with enough books to fill a library. The king welcomed them home personally, pleased for a short time. He then called his wise men before him and explained that he couldn't use the library. He wanted all the information condensed into one book. Something he could use.

The wise men went to work with their scribes and similar to a miracle they completed the task in one year. The king was proudly presented with a 100 pound book which was a condensed version of the entire fly fishing knowledge in the world. He was pleased but not for long. The wise men were once again brought to the great hall. The king told them that he had run out of patience. How could this 100 pound book be put to any practical use? He needed something more condensed.

He was the King and wanted the entire fly fishing knowledge in the world on one piece of paper. If it was not produced all the wise men and their scribes would be executed. However as a fair and just king, they would be given 30 days.

On the 29th day the wisest of the wise men wrote down a 9 word phrase on the scroll. He assured the others that the king being fair, just and wise would accept this. The other wise men thought this old man had lost his mind, for what had been asked was impossible. The king was so passionate about fly fishing that they would all surely be executed.

The day of the event was finally upon us. The executioners were sharpening their axes when the king called the leader of the wise men before him. He asked if they had available what had been requested.

The leader of the wise men presented the king with the beautiful scroll containing the 9 word phrase. The king read the words and then thought for a moment. Finally he spoke and all listened. There would be no execution.

Everything had been made clear to him by his greatest treasure, the wise men. They had led him out of the darkness and into the light forever more.

The king now understood his purpose and how he could best benefit his entire people and continue to live in their hearts long after death had claimed him. Instead of a very large funeral there was a huge celebration. All the wise men and scribes lived long and happy lives and everyone throughout the land prospered.

The entire kingdom lived their lives by the words on the scroll. The 9 words are: THERE IS NO SUCH THING AS A FREE LUNCH.

I promise there will be no regrets of the time invested learning about fly fishing no matter how far you pursue it. You will be paid back many times over with personal satisfaction. Fly fishing is so multi faceted that it's even fun when you aren't actually fishing.

There's fly tying, fly casting, riggings and knots, extensive reading material, ichthyology, biology, habitat enhancement and protection, water quality testing, photography, planning that long thought about trip or thinking of that special place that has given so much enjoyment.

Fly fishing usually occurs in beautiful places. There are artists who share by painting, writers who share their experiences, poets who share their insights, fishing guides who share their ability and knowledge for catching fish along with good fishermen or fisherwomen who share what they know so that others may enjoy the outdoors in the same manner as they.

To me, the definition of Fly Fishing is: The adjusted blended of many learned skills and pieces of information to meet ever changing brook, stream, river, pond, lake or salt challenges by making calculated presentations and or manipulations with an offering (based upon experience, knowledge and observation) in a way which will be accepted as food or activate a reflex response.

Fly fishing can be the saving of a highly pressured executive, a garage mechanic's passion, a working girl's recreation or a ballerina's delight. Fly fishing can be enjoyed by everyone to the level they wish to invest.

************

# Trout Fishing Insights

Twenty years of experience guiding on the challenging Upper Connecticut River and fishing many different streams in New Hampshire, Vermont and New York enable this chapter. Many of the fly fishing techniques given can be successfully adapted to spinning using lures, plugs or bait.

## Demystifying Streamborn Emerging Insects

There are numerous different techniques and riggings in river fishing for trout. Usually this depends upon what the trout are feeding on at that particular moment, what level (top, middle or bottom) and the river conditions (low water, high water, stained water, lightly stained water, perfect conditions, etc).

Trout will feed on different food items such as sculpins, leeches, dragon flies, damsel flies, Dobson flies (hellgrammites), crane flies, terrestrials such as worms, beetles, ants, hoppers, mice, baby birds and bait fish, chubs and smaller trout, etc and at times can become selective to one or more. However the four food forms constantly utilized by most river trout for food when available are caddis flies, mayflies, diptera (midges) and stoneflies.

The ideal conditions upon arriving at your favorite stream or river is when trout are exposing themselves in good numbers while feeding on or near the surface. This usually means a hatch is underway. For the best success in deceiving trout, you will need to offer them a close imitation of the food item they are feeding on at that time. Most fishermen (or women) are aware of this but may encounter frustration by not being able to hook up while fish are showing all around them. They are probably missing the boat by not realizing that the trout may be taking a smaller insect in the surface film or keyed upon a specific stage of insect - mayfly, caddis or diptera, under or in the layer just below the surface. Trout will develop a preference for a particular stage of insect during a hatch, especially on hard fished public water or long placid pools and flats. Allow me to explain.

Most trout feeding during an emergence will focus on the stage of insect which at that particular moment offers the most food mass. This feeding relates to OFT - Optimal Foraging Theory, which means all creatures must consume more calories than the energy expended in that food items capture or they will perish. Through repeated feedings, trout have become masters of energy efficient feeding. They consider feeding on the changing stages of an insect that have the most food mass at that time as a safe reliable food source. This gives them the most calorie intake for the least energy expended. It is more energy efficient for them to feed in this manner than to move to and fro consuming all food forms.

Imagine a large pool on your favorite stream or river. Most large pools will usually have at least a few subtle currents located in different parts which flow through. The greater portion of hatching insects above and in this pool will funnel themselves into these current lanes ( I like to refer to them as feeding lanes). This happens on all moving water that holds trout and is where you will find them lined up like cattle at a feeding trough. It is extremely energy efficient for them to casually feed in the above mentioned manner. The slow moving current is similar to a Lazy Susan bringing the food to them. They need only to hold position and casually tip their head up and sip an insect or insects from the film.

You may notice the dorsal or tail slowly moving as they feed and maybe a small or larger upwelling caused by a trout. This means a food item has been taken in or just below the surface film. Usually this rise form indicates an emerging insect. A trout head, nose, dorsal or tail casually breaking the surface may mean the taking of an insect on top, in or just under the surface film. This is usually associated with smaller insects. If an air bubble shows itself near a feeding trout it is a clue that they are taking insects from the surface. An erratic splashy type of rise indicates a caddis or larger mayfly or stonefly.

Successfully fishing to pods of rising or showing trout is a scenario sought after by huge numbers of fly fishermen all over the world. A favorite technique is to position the boat 40 to 50 feet upstream of the pod or single riser with the anchor down. Wait a few minutes for them to resume active rising again. Have a drink – relax.

Cast across and downstream on a 45 degree angle two thirds of the distance between you and the fish and far to the side. Pull the fly into the feeding lane of the target riser. Allow a drag free drift with the fly reaching the trout's position first before the leader. Use a sequence of mends called stack mending or lift the rod in many short abrupt motions while allowing line to pass through, thus accomplishing the same thing. The fly should not stop its drag free drift before or near the position of the trout. Be careful when mending to not influence the fly or the drag free drift especially when near the trout. Allow the drift to continue through the trout to a few feet below before picking up. Be careful not to spook the target.

Make the same cast again but this time add a few subtle twitches just before reaching the position of the trout, then allow the fly to continue through drag free. The strike will come as a visible take or splash. It may also be an appearance and slight movement of the dorsal or head where you perceive the fly to be. Wait a second and then gently lift the rod towards a 45 degree angle until resistance is felt.

This gently applied tension will be enough to set the hook with the small fly and light leader you will more than likely be using in this scenario. Flies in the 18 and smaller size with 6x or less tippets are often necessary. If the hatch is of larger flies in the 12 to 16 range a bit more of a hookset can be used because a 4 or 5x leader will instead be in play. The technique remains the same.

A boil type rise may appear just before or while the nymph emerges through the back of its thorax or as it tries to shake free of its attached shuck. A soft hackle or a soft hackle with a small nymph attached to the bend with a one foot tippet is an excellent way to imitate an emerging insect.

Good basic nymph choices in this situation are Pheasant Tail, Hares Ear, Prince or a Copper John in sizes 16 to 20. Allow this to drift drag free to the trout. If no strike let it drift drag free a few feet below and then repeat. This time give the fly a few abrupt twitches near the trout then allow a foot of drag free drift and then more abrupt twitches. You are imitating the emerging insects below the surface. Hold on. The strikes can usually be hard and fast with this method. Be ready to set the hook and then give line, especially if hooked to a good fish. These techniques can be adapted for wading by fly fishing and spinning anglers.

In addition to emerging insects, a movement of caddis, mayflies, diptera (true midges) and stonefly nymphs occurs for a short period every day called Biological Drift.

This entails insects releasing hold of the stream bottom and drifting up to 15 feet and then reattaching or seeking new cover. The movement takes place near sunrise and sunset and to a smaller extent around midnight. The insects do this to distribute themselves evenly throughout a stream and to not place their entire mass in any one area, giving a better chance for the most to survive to emerge and to also prevent overcrowding. This overcrowding will eventually lead to mass predation by larger stream insects. The trout are aware of biological drift and feed heavily at these times on sub surface insects. That is why fishing may pick up for a short while and then drop off again especially within an hour or two of sunrise or sunset. Quite often, it is Biological Drift which creates this bite.

Let's follow the progression of emerging mayflies and a similar emergence by caddis and diptera. They are first available to trout near the bottom of the stream as a nymph. When ready to emerge they make their way up to the elastic like meniscus called the surface film (surface). The insect's difficulty in breaking through the surface film to become airborne is similar to a human pushing through 4 feet of sand. No simple task. Then the insect begins to literally crawl out of the back of its thorax. This stage is called an emerger.

The insect is very susceptible to consumption by trout at this time. Huge quantities of vulnerable insects during this stage can be efficiently sipped from the surface film. If the insect gets wet it will prevent or delay successful emergence. Although trout, birds and other predators inflict a heavy toll upon these hatching insects, many still survive, mate and deposit eggs back into the water body insuring the continuation of the species. Many do not make it and are consumed by trout and other fish species as cripples or stillborn. Isn't it ironic that after spending their entire lives as a sub aquatic nymph below the surface in an aquatic environment, their very existence and purpose upon emergence depends on not getting wet.

The next stage is the captive dun. This is when the insect has emerged but may be still stuck to the shuck. Usually they will twitch violently trying to free themselves. This is another good stage to imitate. Then the insect is finally rid of its shuck, wings are damp and a low silhouette is present on the surface. This is called the transitional dun. When feeding on this and all the preceding stages the trout knows through prior experience that they have time and usually can casually feed without fear of the insect flying away causing wasted energy.

Not so with the next stage. This stage is called the dun. This is when the insect is fully emerged, free of its shuck and high riding on the surface with upright wings. They can now fly away at any moment. Perhaps you have seen a trout expending energy on an escaping insect which became airborne. A trout will venture into the outside world beyond the surface to take an insect if sufficient insect mass warrants it or if there is no hatch or other insects available. Individuals may feed on the occasional insect, especially smaller trout. Although many of the smaller mayflies will emerge, molt, and mate within an hour or two most take 24 hours.

The next and final stage is called a spinner. Upon mating the sought after females, (spinners) with their high calorie content eggs fall upon the surface to deposit them. Some will make their way down submerged logs and rocks or even dive under in order to deposit those eggs. These female spinners (and to a smaller extent male spinners) offer another feeding opportunity.

For most northeast streams or rivers, many different insects will begin actively hatching sometime in March and continue through to October, November and even into December. This depends upon water temperature and to some extent the amount of daylight in a 24 hour period. During the course of a season these flies will offer trout many feeding opportunities with different types of insects hatching at different times of the day.

A trout may only accept a specific stage of insect near but not on the surface. Lack of surface action may place your best chances with a sub surface nymph drifted close to the bottom or a streamer fished with a sink tip or a floating line with or without shot for depth control. Sometimes a trout will only accept a specific stage of insect near the bottom of the stream or on its way to the surface.

Trout opportunity for both surface and sub surface exist throughout all different water types of a river system. The fishing is more diverse than pursuing them on the long flats and pools. A trout will come up in fast pocket water to accept an offering but the take will be with less finesse than on a pool or flat. They have less time to view the insects. A decision to take or not needs to be quickly made and carried out.

A good technique is to position above a rapid, riffle or run containing brisk pocket water. Skitter a floating Elk Hair Caddis through the many created mini pools from above.

Sometimes the trout will take a drag free drift and sometimes they like it skittered. This is a fun and easy way to fish. A soft hackle, nymph or combination of the two is another good choice using a floating line with or without weight and an indicator. Weight will allow a deeper presentation. Try skittering a 14 or 16 Elk Hair Caddis from above, through brisk pocket water with a small nymph or soft hackle tied to its bend.

The conventional upstream cast to rising trout still has its place when the conditions are right. When possible, I prefer to make a downstream or down and across presentation because the fly reaches the trout's position before the leader and fly line affording less of a chance to spook them.

Two of very important line manipulations in fly fishing are the Reach Cast, Mending or Stack Mending. Stack Mending is the same as mending. Instead of one or two mends a continuation of mends is executed to allow the fly to either gain depth or achieve a longer drag free drift.

The Reach Cast is the reaching of the rod to the left or right near the end of the cast and then move the rod tip back to the side several feet before the line lands. The goal of the reach cast is to delay drag while giving those few extra seconds of drag free drift. This can be accomplished by making a cast and then extend the rod while pulling several feet of line to the side in the same manner. A drag free drift is created during the few seconds it takes the current to absorb the slack line. The delay of the currents influence in straightening the fly line affords the drag free drift.

When the slack line is eliminated by the current, drag begins to occur. Usually an imitation of a nymph, emerging nymph, floating nymph, emerger, captive dun, transitional dun, high riding dun or spinner will save the day. Fish two different stages at a time and let the trout tell you what they want at that moment. The preference can change as the hatch progresses or another insect begins hatching in greater numbers. That is what offers the greatest challenge. If we could go out and fish for showing trout with the same fly every time and receive a strike on every cast it would lose its magic.

For a two fly rig I simply tie a 10 to 12 inch tippet to the bend of the first fly. For smaller flies 18 – 24 thread the first fly then tie on a 1 to two foot tippet to the end of the line. The knot will stop the fly from sliding beyond it. Now tie on the second fly to the end of the tippet.

When fishing on or near the surface use 3x for fly sizes 6-8, 4x for sizes 10 to 12, 5x for sizes 14 to 16, 6x for 18 to 20 and 7x for 22 to 24.

## Suggested Styles of Flies to Match the Hatch
FLOATING NYMPH – mole fur or dun cdc is added to the top of the thorax region and fished in or just under the surface film to rising fish. Sizes 12 - 24.

EMERGER – Soft Hackle or cdc emerger -This is a great fly by itself or with a nymph tied to the bend with a 10 – 12 inch tippet. Sizes 12 - 20.

CAPTIVE DUN – Compara-dun with a Z-lon or Antron shuck - light medium or dark dun cdc or elk can be used for wing – this is a style fly used for challenging trout which is very effective in sizes from 12 to 24.

TRANSITIONAL DUN – Compara-dun – light, medium, or dark dun cdc or elk is used for wing with the wing slanted downward across the back. The tails are splayed. Use sizes 12 to 24. Good fly for the beginning of the hatch, especially if the flies appear flush in the film instead of high riding. Great fly for challenging trout.

DUN – Classic Catskill style with cock hackles tail and hackle. Wood duck wings or mallard for most ties. Good fly when the hatch is underway with insects seen floating high on the surface. Sizes 12 to 24. Hackle can be clipped below the body to present a flush in the film imitation similar to the transitional dun.

SPINNER – Thin body and splayed tails. Wings can be clipped variant hackle top and bottom or cdc feathers or small full hen feathers the color of the natural wing tied in on each side of the fly - usually wings are dark, light or medium dun or a light cream or creamy yellow. Sizes 12 – 24.

## A Few Other Style Flies to Consider
1. Parachutes, 12 - 24. Good fly for difficult trout
2. Elk Hair Caddis, 12 -24. Surface caddis imitation.

3. Stimulator, 10 – 14. Good searching pattern & stone-fly imitation.
4. Madam X, 10 – 14 . Good searching pattern & stone-fly imitation.
5. Griffiths Gnat, 18 – 24. Great small fly.
6. Orange Asher, 18 – 24. Great small fly.
7. Hoppers, 8 – 16. Good fly from mid August thru September

## Other Fly Fishing Options
There will be times there is little or no surface activity. There are options.

1. Nymph
2. Streamer
3. Attractor Flies

### Nymphs
Nymphs can be fished one or two at a time with or without a strike indicator on a floating line. When rigging an indicator (small bobber) or fishing any nymph, try to use as little lead free shot as needed to accomplish sinking the fly to the desired depth. The shot is placed 10 to 12 inches above the nymph. Place the indicator 1-1/2 times the depth of the water above the shot. As the depth changes adjust the indicator to the proper depth.

A drag free drift is desired. To accomplish this, use rod and line manipulations. Most casts will have little or no fly line touching the water. Cast the fly slightly upstream. As the nymph hits the water your rod should be pointed low and towards the fly. Gradually lift the rod and retrieve line with the speed of the current until held high overhead as the offering drifts in front of your position, all the while try to execute a drag-free drift with the offering near the bottom. (Watching the indicator helps greatly in this goal). Now lower the rod, slowly and slightly pivot your body towards downstream. Follow the fly with the rod as it passes. Watch the indicator while trying to accomplish keeping it floating drag free.

Set the hook when an unnatural movement of the indicator occurs. Reach a little at the end, allowing a few extra drag free feet. Switching rod hands at this time can sometimes accomplish this depending on which way the current is flowing and which hand is holding the rod.

When not using an indicator, still place the shot 10 to 12 inches above the fly. If you are concentrating more on the swing at the end of the float the shot should be placed 2 to 4 feet above the fly for a more natural swing.

For nymphs I will use from 3x to 6x tippet, depending on the fly used and the conditions. For stained water use a heavier tippet otherwise a good starting point is fly sizes 2 - 6 use 3x, sizes 8 -12 use 4x, sizes 14 – 16 use 5x, sizes 18 – 20 use 6x, and sizes 22 – 24 use 7x.

### Streamers:
A streamer may be fished effectively with a floating line with or without shot, depending on the depth desired for the presentation. Many folks use a very fast sinking sink tip fly line with a 10 15 foot sinking head integrated into a floating running line. Use a short leader with this set up, seldom over 5 feet in length. A longer leader will allow the fly to buoy upward and not fol-

low the path of the sinking portion. This negates the effectiveness of the sink tip.

One of the many techniques I use with this line is to hold position in my drift boat by dropping anchor above a good run I know to hold numbers of trout. My guests will make angled casts above the run, add a few mends for depth and allow the streamer to swing through productive water slightly downstream. The boat is slowly worked downstream while allowing the swinging of streamers through new water until we start hitting fish.

It is also important to let the streamer hold for a few seconds at the end of the swing. That is when the fly begins to come off the bottom and gain a bit more velocity imitating an escaping insect or stressed or wounded baitfish. (This also holds true for spinning anglers using spinners, plugs or bait.)

It may help to hold a few strips of line in hand to release as the swing starts near the end of the drift and through the productive target. This softens the abruptness of the swinging fly which can sometimes bring more strikes. Hand twitching the line or rod during the swing can also be a triggering factor.

Try retrieving the streamer half way back after the swing completes. Then release the line while feeding out several additional strips of line from the reel. This allows fishing a little farther downstream than the previous swinging cast. Keep in touch with the fly as it drifts downstream, then slowly retrieve. Try this a few times and it may pick up a bonus fish.

Another good technique when using streamers with a sink tip is to cast towards the bank or good looking structure, make several strips then recast. A lot of water can be quickly covered this way while giving aggressive trout an opportunity to take the fly.

Through a slow moving pool or flat the person in the rear of the boat has the option of casting to the bank allowing the streamer to swing behind the boat.

Another effective technique is to fish the streamer like a nymph, with shot, through runs and rapids. Use from 4x to 2x tippet. In stained water use 2x, during low clear water 4x and for most conditions, 3x. This is a good starting point for tippet choice when pursuing stream, river and pond trout.

## Recommended Spinning Offerings for Trout:

### Spinners:
PANTHER MARTIN - 1/8 to 1/16 ounce. Black Body with Yellow Dots, Yellow Body with Orange Dots.

MEPPS AGLIA - Undressed - 1/6 ounce. Gold Blade, Silver Blade.

BLUE FOX VIBRAX - 1/8 or 1/6 ounce. Silver Blade, Gold Blade, Rainbow Trout.

### Rapalas:
FLOATING RAPALA - number 5, 7 and 9. Silver and Black, Rainbow Trout, Gold, Perch.

SINKING RAPALA - number 3, 5 & 7. Silver and Black, Gold, Rainbow .

X RAP RAPALA - 2-1/2 and 3-1/8 inch. Rainbow, Olive, Silver and Red

RAPALA JOINTED SHAD RAP - 2 inch. Silver.

LUHR JENSEN HOT SHOT - Size 50. Black Scale, Brown Trout, Green Pirate, Rainbow Trout,

REBEL WEE CRAWFISH - 1/5 ounce. Brown Crawfish, Olive Crawfish.

LITTLE CLEO SPOON - 1/8 and 1/6 ounce. Gold.

PHOEBE SPOON - 1/12, 1/8 and 1/6 ounce . Gold.

LUHR JENSEN SUPER DUPER - 1/8 and 1/6 ounce. Silver/Red Head and Gold/Red Head.

*************

# Guiding and Shared Experiences

This sounds like a great way to make a living, doesn't it? You work in the beautiful outdoors while observing acts and sounds of nature encountered by most only on the Discovery Channel. Become your own person and make good money. Respect yourself while also earning the respect of others. There is another side you may consider.

It takes years of passion, dedication and hard work along with limitless patience with guests. There is a lot more to it than just being a good fisherman yourself. You need to be able to translate that safely and intelligently to guests of many different fishing abilities in a way which informs while always demonstrating the highest degree of respect. Be ready to invest years of hard work, experience and research to become competent to guide someone professionally.

You must possess an understanding of fish behavior for the pursued species under many different conditions, learn and master the many different techniques and offerings which will be used for the target species and when to use each one along with being able to translate this knowledge so that others may benefit by being able to hook, play and land fish themselves, no matter their level of fishing competence.

Whatever your level of expertise, perspective guests will not be beating your door down. It is important to properly advertise or be hooked up with a busy outfitter who will recommend your services or both. The reality for most is, it will still take years to build a guiding business where a person can support themselves or you must be very lucky and find yourself connected with the right people who can help.

If you are fortunate in this area it will still be imperative to possess people skills under pressure and be extremely accomplished in the chosen area of guiding. A few guiding options are pond, lake, ocean, estuary, brook, stream and river. There is fly fishing, spinning, level wind, using flies, bait, hardware or soft plastics. Target species are too many to be mentioned with most having different environments which will require different techniques, at different depths, using different gear with different offerings at different levels at different times under different conditions.

My game is operating a drift boat in a freshwater river while pursuing smallmouth bass and trout. It is imperative to be in very good physical condition because of all the rowing. The easy way out is to guide shoreline or wading anglers. Although not offering the satisfaction of reaching all the best fish catching spots or the pride in gaining the ability through hard work to navigate the rivers challenges successfully, there are no 9 foot oars attached to the wading guide.

Sometimes those oars can get extremely heavy during a 9 – 10 hour day. This is especially true when it is necessary to hold in current for long  periods enabling your guests to reach feeding trout. On those days when the wind is brisk and blowing up river through the half to mile long pools and flats, it is a bear to push your guest downstream with those same oars.

When floating a river there is a commitment made at the beginning of each float. That commitment is you cannot finish the float until the takeout. This is where the pre-arranged vehicle to take out your raft, flat bottom, drift boat, canoe or kayak is located. A wading guide can wade in or out at many of the productive areas without the same commitment.

On the plus side it is a totally different experience when drifting a river. It is a bit of an adventure putting in at point A and floating to a pre determined point B. Your outing is limited to the chosen section however the entire river in this space is at your beck and call. Also, many fishermen (or women) cannot or prefer not to wade or bank fish. A drift boat float enables these folks to safely enjoy a unique outdoor experience.

An experienced operator can navigate so their guests can fish all the productive water and hold the boat a comfortable casting distance enabling guests to safely cast to those hard to reach from shore places. There is so much more involved in becoming a successful drift boat operator as compared to a wading guide. You are responsible for providing a comfortable and safe fishing platform for your clients to fish from while putting them at the best casting position to reach feeding fish at every opportunity throughout the day.

A drift boat guide must be aware when to offer casting and fishing suggestions which can help their guests to be more successful throughout their day as well as making fly or lure suggestions, retrieve rate, depth and manipulations which will afford them the best chance for success. The bottom line is every professional drift boat operator and guide who has demonstrated longevity by providing their service for a reasonable amount of time has a great deal of pride in their ability to navigate their guests safely and effectively throughout a day on the river. They will offer every fish catching opportunity possible for that particular day.

I also believe that a drift boat guide has made a much larger commitment to their guests and to themselves as compared to person who offers wading only. McKenzie Drift Boat operators will also pull the boat over to productive wading areas for those who enjoy wading. Split second judgment with good coordination is needed to safely guide on the more challenging rivers.

Most folks need help with fly selection, identifying and

casting to good fish holding structure and managing fly line. You will need to instruct most guests in the execution of the different techniques needed to hook, land and carefully release the challenging fish of New Hampshire's Upper Connecticut River. Join me for a day in the life of an Upper Connecticut River Fishing Guide.

Beep-Beep-Beep-Beep - It's 6 a.m. already. I have to meet two clients in Colebrook, N.H. today at 11 a.m. for a fly fishing float on the Upper C. I shave, shower, dress and then take a look in the mirror. Yeah! Okay! There's a fishing guide. Go over the check list to make sure everything is packed. 7:30 already – time to go. I usually stay up north in a motel for 4 or 5 days at a time but this is a one day trip. A smallmouth float on my home waters tomorrow means driving back after today's float.

I hook up the McKenzie Drift Boat and drive a couple of miles to pick up 91 North and start my 130 mile drive. Anticipation is high because the river is in good shape. A cloudy sky is predicted today with little or no wind. These are great conditions.

The Upper C is a good trout stream. Thousands of trout will be covered today. Maybe a bear will swim across the river in front of us like last week. Upon reaching the shoreline the bear shook like a dog from head to toe to dry itself and then scurried up the bank. We estimated its weight around 250 pounds.

Perhaps the otters will put on a show like the week before. We were fishing under an overhanging maple which provided lots of shade and fish. A family of otters swam right through the area we were fishing. There were two babies and a mother. The mom had something in her mouth. It was another baby. Mother and family moved into shore and climbed up a steep muddy bank. This incline was so steep that one of the babies slid back down into the water. The pup couldn't climb up. The two preceding babies and mother had made the path too slick.

The baby otter started screaming, making ear piercing sounds like a howling puppy. Did the mother otter abandon her pup? This animal had won our sympathy. We were ready to leave the area with the hope that mom would come back in our absence. Then we saw it. About a hundred feet away there was a movement of water similar to a shark closing in on its prey, headed towards the baby otter.. About 5 feet from its target a huge otter head broke water, looked around carefully observing us and then sounded.

She resurfaced again just behind and above the baby, appearing with the profile of a cobra. She was enormous by comparison. The mom otter reached down and grabbed the little one behind the neck and lifted it out of the water, like a mother cat carrying a kitten. She stared at us for a few seconds with the baby in her mouth, before diving under. Their progress was observed by the wake which followed them.

We may see bear, beaver, deer, ducks, eagles, fox, hawks, kingfishers, moose, ospreys, otter, turtles or who knows what else or when. There is no set script.

While still thinking of past clients there's a reflection of some of the good and bad decisions made. I tell myself all decisions today will be the right ones. Thoughts direct towards developing a strategy for the choice of rods, lines, flies and techniques.

Here's Lancaster, N.H. already – another 35 miles. A left onto Rte. 3 North and only a half hour to Colebrook, N.H. Should we begin with dries, emergers, nymphs or streamers? These are the questions asked of myself as the distance to the boat launch lessens. Here is Colebrook already and right on schedule. Its 10 a.m. That gives me an hour to launch and set up a couple of rods.

I reflect to last weeks float. There was an isolated, torrential thunder storm here just two hours before I arrived, making the river muddy and not fishable. What a bad break. It was so difficult for me to share the bad news with my guests. I mention to Les that the White River, about 100 miles south, was running clear. We would have to wade but the fish were there and the conditions were right, for good action. They both agreed after viewing the chocolate colored river that the Upper C was not fishable. The guys expressed confidence in me and would follow any suggestions.

We began our two hour trip back to the White River. They were on the water and fishing by 1:30. Lady luck was shinning for us as we fished the right water and used the correct flies. Greg (son) and Les caught and released at least 50 beautiful wild trout - rainbows and browns. Greg, a twenty year old college student, also caught and released a vibrant 18 inch brown. All on surface flies. Good fishing by any standard.

The next day, at their request, I made it possible for them to experience a very enjoyable type of fly fishing. We went after smallmouth bass with my drift boat on a scenic and productive section of the Connecticut River. The area we fished is below Wilder Dam. Les and Greg were surprised that a hundred and thirty miles to the north this same river was running the color of chocolate milk yet was clear here, downstream. I explained the reason was the many dams acted like power pools, usually releasing water to accommodate power demands. Today the releases were working to our benefit. Greg caught a few smallmouth but Les, his dad, was dominating and having a ball. The year before the shoe was on the other foot with Greg catching many more fish and never missing the opportunity to remind his dad. We ended this trip at dusk with Greg hooking, landing and releasing the fish of the day, a trophy smallmouth close to five pounds while fly fishing with a Size 4 - Number 41 - Gaines Dixie Devil Popper. The big bass fought us hard for close to ten minutes with explosive jumps and hard runs. Who said big bass do not jump! This was a great end to a fun day.

Les and Greg thanked me as we said goodbyes. They brought notice to the fact that yesterday morning they perceived a huge disappointment with the stained river conditions. Experience and patience turned their vacation around and enabled them to share two great days and many fond memories. The wonderful feeling of contentment then is also present now.

Not all trips end on such a positive note, reflecting to a float three weeks ago. I am not impressed when a person communicates that he or she is an expert or highly skilled fisherman. To myself, I will usually say, Oh boy! Here we go again. The Upper C. at times can be extremely unforgiving of sloppy casting, poor rod and line manipulations, improper fly selection or lack of concentration. On more than one occasion, I have had a self proclaimed expert not know what a reach cast was and have a 40 foot casting limit.

One barely average, so called highly experienced fly fisherman guest, told me that he wasn't aware of the reach cast but if he didn't hear of it, it wasn't important. This particular gentleman had a 50 foot casting limit which under most conditions is more than enough. The glitch is when working a fish he would constantly be a foot or two short with the cast. I quietly slid the boat a little closer for the next fish but he was a foot or two short. I slid a little closer for the next fish with the same results. Finally, I stalked to within 25 feet away from a surface feeding trout but the fly still fell a foot short with the usual line slap. That was frustrating. When he was able to receive a strike the set was usually non existent.

I changed flies for him to a soft hackle with a nymph dropper. I explained that the trout were not willing to come to the surface to take a fly today (A bit of a fib). The fish are usually more inclined to move a little more to aggressively take an offering with this combination as compared to a surface fly, especially when he twitched it a little. I set up 50 feet above a pod of rising fish. He cast to the side and upstream of the pod, brought the fly into the feed lane and then mended down to the feeding trout drag free with the fly reaching the fish ahead of the leader. This adjustment enabled us to catch our share throughout the rest of the float. I was cordial the entire day and was able to maintain a positive experience even though he was a difficult person to guide.

On the other side of the coin I have floated with discrete folks who have possessed all the attributes of an expert, if there is such a thing, but never referred to themselves as such. The best compliment one fly fisherman can give to another is to acknowledge their competence as being a "Good Fisherman".

I focus back to the present. The boat is ready, the equipment is organized and ready to go. I do not see any rising trout so two rods were rigged with a nymph, soft hackle, shot and indicator. I make a cast upstream, raise the rod as the fly drifts back to me then slowly lower it with the speed of the current while pointing my rod tip at the indicator. There, a slight movement of the indicator. I raise the rod quickly and a 12 inch rainbow leaps from the water. The trout is quickly played and released. That's it for me. I don't want to work these fish.

11 AM and here they are right on time. Jim booked the trip and I notice right away that he is very respectful towards Bill, his boss. They are both executives seeking a temporary reprieve from the real world. My perception is Bill holds the key to Jim's future.

I suggest for Bill to take the front casting position. It is my experience that the person in front of the boat will usually receive a few more strikes during a float, especially if they can place their fly in the right places. I plan to discretely help Bill accomplish this along with suggestions for manipulations of the fly, if necessary. It is my perception that Jim would like Bill to do well.

Nine hours later and as it turns out, it is another good day on the river. They were decent fly fishermen which made my job much easier.

We started out fishing a floating line with a 5x tippet while using small pheasant tail nymph trailers tied to a hare's ear soft hackle. The final few hours allowed us to cast to rising trout. They devoured our size 16 pale evening dun imitations with abandon.

Bill landed an 18 inch brown while losing one just as large to a blow down (underwater tree). Jim landed a gorgeous, electric 16 inch rainbow, which left little doubt of its origin, wild fish, born and raised in the river. This trout jumped close to a dozen times. The trout today were accommodating, full of electricity and hard fighting. We did well, landing around twenty and losing about the same. Water temp was 61 with a light breeze and cloudy. The hatch was on, my guests were up for it and the trout were willing. A great day.

We float by a herd of dairy cows standing motionless like statues on the bank. All eyes are upon us. We have met many times before with the same reception. It is less than a quarter mile to the take out and the end of a fine day for my guests. Bill picks up a nice 13 inch rainbow and Jim follows suit just before we finish. We chat and then goodbyes are shared before I start the 3 plus hour ride home.

It takes longer because a slower speed with extreme caution must prevail because of all the moose encountered – many standing in the middle of the road. I flash back to the strategies and techniques which proved to be successful today. Every detail is gone over with the objective of applying this information in solving future stream challenges. There is no such thing as a problem. There are only challenges. Each challenge presents me with an opportunity to create a solution. I enjoy reflecting upon past floats before and after a long day on the Upper C. It helps to analyze them thus better preparing myself for future trips.

There's 91 south. It's only another hour to White River Junction. I think about the husband and wife from Massachusetts who booked last season. The husband liked to fish while my first perception of the wife was that she hoped for the day to pass as quickly and painlessly as possible.

It wasn't long before she was sharing a warm, genuine, smile. We lost count of the trout Lisa caught that day. Both of us picked on her husband Bob when she caught and released a 4 pound rainbow. Lisa told her husband that it would take 4 of yours to equal one of mine. I quickly mentioned to Bob that I was glad his wife was with us because I needed to count on someone to land a big fish. This comment brought another chuckle as well as another ear to ear grin from Lisa. We had a lot of fun that day. Thank goodness the fish were on.

How about last years honeymoon couple from Maryland? The bride was in her high sixties and the groom his low seventies. They were both very energetic. It seemed like I was out with a couple of college kids. We were river fishing in my McKenzie drift boat for small-mouth bass on the same river only 140 miles to the south.

The fish were willing, explosive striking and high jumping. My clients caught and released at least 15 large smallmouth and lost just as many to the antics they are famous for. Carl and Louise had a honeymoon ball. I feel good just thinking about them.

The father and son earlier this season from Connecticut couldn't believe their eyes when a large, aggressive cow moose and her yearling blocked our floating path, on the Upper C. She stood her ground between us and her baby in a shallow section of river for over 30 minutes, preventing the continuing of our float. The youngster finally grew tired of this game and crossed the river. Mom followed close behind enabling us to continue our float. This experience along with the pictures taken put the final touches on a good trip for Bill and Alex.

While driving other companions upstream at the end of a float in early June we saw a yearling moose standing in the middle of the road. It was late May. The mother moose push their young ones away at this time of the year. The youngsters are usually disoriented. I had to completely stop about 3 feet from the yearling to slowly pass in the other lane. The young moose began to run next to the passenger side about 2 feet from my open window. He continued with us for about 100 yards. We were looking out the window, a couple of feet away, at the head of moose, running along next to us, bobbing up and down. It was like the animal channel coming to life. The clomping hooves provided the sound effects. My guests loved it.

I remember taking out a family from Florida, on a float trip for trout, on the Upper C, a couple of years back. It was a husband, wife and two children. Originally, just the father and eleven year old son were scheduled. When we met the entire family was ready to float and fish. I made a few adjustments and was able to make this happen for them.

The son and thirteen year old daughter were both very well mannered. They had not held a fly rod in their hands before and wanted to fly fish along with their dad and mom. This is a challenge which I have willingly accepted many times in the past. What I am about is helping folks to enjoy the outdoors in a way they would not be able to on their own.

What better opportunity to accomplish this than with people who get very little chance to spend time outdoors but have a yearning to do so. The trout were fairly receptive this particular day. We were able to figure out what insect they were feeding on and its particular stage of development. They took turns fishing two at a time. My guests listened to all suggestions while doing their best. It was a beautiful day, the trout were willing and the folks were happy. We caught a lot of fish that day, with a few reaching the 14 - 15 inch range. What fishing guide could ask for more? These beginner fly fishermen told me they had one of the coolest experiences of their lives. We floated the river about 8 hours finishing at dusk. That wonderful feeling then is also with me now. It's why I guide.

Dave, a good friend and I have enjoyed numerous smallmouth and trout float experiences together. This enables staying in touch with the fishing for my clients during days off. He brings his drift boat when I have a float the next day, allowing me to keep my boat set up and clean for that days fishing. We usually take turns switching from rowing to fishing every couple of fish. This keeps each other sharp especially with the shared critique or compliments depending on the days performance. It's a great way to be on top of my game and be able to execute for my guests when necessary.

My thoughts travel a few weeks ago to one of the many floats on the Upper Connecticut with Tom and Walter, two good fly fisherman. We started this early June day catching fish on a paralep imitation (Blue Quill) even though there was a good Hendrickson hatch.

The trout were keyed into these smaller flies because they were so abundant. Tom picked up on it. We landed a half dozen nice fish before the rain began, heavier and heavier, but still we caught trout consistently. Then it began to torrential downpour even though all weather reports called for only brief showers. This was the Upper Connecticut River.

We knew that on many occasions during the summer, sometimes without warning, fast moving violent systems will move through the region. We put on our rain gear. It was a couple of hours into the float so we continued to fish hard, all suspecting the worse but for us negativity wasn't part of our thought process, at least not at that point.

This changed. The heavy rain continued. The runoff began to stain the water and put the trout down (they stopped feeding) and it all began with an occasional shower forecast for the day. The last 6 hours gave up two hard earned fish as the torrential downpour refused to let up. The torrential downpour refused to let up. (Yes, the heavy rain we experienced was so intense it needed to be mentioned more than once). We finished the float resembling drowned rats. This was a tough day. The drive home was long, reflecting and disappointing. The feeling of satisfaction was absent.

There were other trips my guests and I were into fish but violent systems containing thunder & lighting forced us to leave the boat and wait it out in our rain gear on shore. Sometimes these systems would last 15 minutes, sometimes an hour, and sometimes two or three hours or longer.

I remember a trip with Adam, Ted & Ben and another with Bill & Mike. We waited on the bank covered with rain gear, watching trout rise while creatively encouraging the system to pass. On each of these occasions we were able to do very well after the storm passed. One moment the prospects for continued fishing looked bleak and gloomy with a dark ominous sky, wind, cold rain and thunder and lightning. Twenty minutes later, our entire being seemed to be warmed by a welcomed old friend, the sun, the stopping of the wind and rain and feeding trout. The generous double rainbow on each occasion was a fine bonus. The upper river is know for numerous quick moving violent weather systems pushing through.

A float with Bill and Wayne ended differently. It found us working hard all day for 5 or 6 trout, one a beautiful 17 inch rainbow. It was deceived, well played, landed and gently released by Wayne. From previous floats, I knew that they were in for a treat the last couple of hours. About an hour and a half before dusk we set up just above a huge pod of trout, containing numerous big fish and just starting to rise. They fed heavily near the surface on caddis and little yellow olive stoneflies. Before we could make the first cast there was a flash of lighting. Then there it was and moving on us fast. An enormous weather system quickly moving in from over the top of the local mountain. It's Vermont's version of Mount Monadnock. Each approaching weather system shows at the top of the mountain before, a few moments later, reaching the surrounding area.

This system resembled what the end of the world might look like. I had to immediately row into shore, we suited up with rain gear and prepared to wait it out. I could not see across the river which was less than 70 feet away. Less than 60 seconds passed before this system was on us, bringing torrential rain and thunder you could feel vibrate throughout your body and hear a half dozen times as it echoed through the mountains and valleys. The thunder was similar to fireworks only much more powerful and much louder. The lightning lit up the sky branching out into numerous fork-like strikes.

We waited for over an hour while watching big trout rise with abandon. It was now 9 P.M. I reluctantly made our way to the boat take out about a mile away. All the trout had stopped rising by now but the violent weather continued. It was a most disheartening experience for my guests but even more so for myself. The bad weather lasted most the night, putting the river out of shape for a few days. Although I did a good job, the wonderful feeling of contentment is absent when thinking of that float. If we only had another hour before that system engulfed us, I could have been part of a lifelong memorable experience for those gentlemen.

Then there is the float just last week for smallmouth. My guest landed a beautiful 5 plus pound fish near the end of a very good day. While releasing the huge smallie after a Boga Grip picture, she made a quick, unexpected head shake. This yanked the Boga out of my hand. We saw the bass in 4 feet of water enabling a try with the net. The fish would have none of this and swam into deeper water – Grip still attached. We looked for 5 minutes and then I decided it was time to move on. Just one more brief look. I definitely did not want to lose the tool but also the thought of a wonderful five pound female dying in this manner was too much to take.

There it was in 8 feet of water. I saw the shiny part of the Boga Grip. My pants, shirt and shoes quickly came off. Thank goodness I occasionally listen to my wife. She constantly lectures me to wear underwear, especially when out in public. Well, I do. My underwear are the colorful boxer type with a look similar to a bathing suit. Once my mind was made up I was in the water in a flash zeroing in on the shiny object. When near the bottom I lost sight of it but with my arms extended I felt the fish.

She slithered through my hands. I reached out and luckily felt the metal and my grip tightened. When I arrived at the surface and passed the Trophy Bass and Boga, before climbing into the boat, my guests began to whoop and holler. A minute later we made a good release with the big girl swimming off on her own. This was a perfect finish for a great day on the river giving a memorable experience for my guests as well as myself. When arriving home the first thing done was to go online to purchase two Boga Floats to attach so this does not happen again.

There have been so many trips over the years and so many different people from places near and far possessing a wide range of fishing skills. One thing they all have in common is they are all good people and it was my pleasure to spend time with each and every one of them. I was not able to produce that great fish catching outing for every float, but 100% effort was given to each party.

I made it a point on those days the fishing was not gangbusters to capitalize on all the other things we experienced on a float. The wildlife, scenery, flora, fauna, helpful fishing information and tips and discrete casting critique was all brought into play to enrich their day and help them towards future outdoor pursuits.

Finally, the sign says White River Junction and its only 1:30 a.m. Another twenty minutes until I arrive home. Damn I feel so content, tired but content. I always feel wonderful like this after sharing a good days fishing.

So you want to be a river fishing guide. Is this line of

work for you? You decide. There's my driveway. I'm home at last. It was another 18 hour day. I have a six hour local smallmouth float reserved for a meeting time of noon tomorrow. My bed looks very inviting.

## Old Friend

On occasion my guests and I experience the disappointment of the one that got away. The following experience took place in upstate New York near the town of Sandy Creek while on a personal fishing vacation.

The heavy rain which brings high water run off came early this year, sometime in early to mid-March. April presented little precipitation, very low water and few steelhead. Finally, towards the third week of April the rains came, causing the rivers and creeks to swell over their banks. These are the conditions that bring in plenty of large, fresh, lake run rainbows often referred to as steelhead.

The only drawback was the larger rivers were at flood stage, muddy and not fishable. The main runs had already taken place in the smaller creeks but it has been my experience that high water could bring in another run of fresh fish. Soon there would not be an opportunity for a personal fishing vacation. It was either now or not go on the spring steelhead trip this year.

I knew of a good creek, an old friend which had shared her secrets and her steelhead with me in the past. Perhaps the high water brought in some fresh fish. This particular water cleared quickly and might be fishable. This fact kept me positive. The larger rivers were not fishable. However on the plus side there were very few fishermen in the area because of the difficult conditions. If I could locate fish there would be little competition. Steelhead can be here today and gone tomorrow. Even if fish were not found, I knew a good time was ahead. Sometimes it is enough to just be part of playing the game.

I arrived at the creek around 1 p.m. The present light rain didn't bother me as waders and rain gear were put on. My outlook greatly improved when I viewed the water conditions. The velocity was intense but she was running lightly stained with fair visibility. The decision was made to leave the net in my truck because it was awkward to carry especially with all the walking ahead. This was a small creek not a larger river. Spiked sandals would be necessary because her rocks are slick. I felt the chances for finding fish were good.

After rigging the 8-1/2 foot 7 weight fly rod, I slowly started working my way downstream while visually scouring every pocket and possible lie. If I spook any fish on the way downstream make sure to mark the area mentally and work it on the way out.

She is a beautiful, fast flowing creek containing an abundance of rapids and pockets with an average depth of 12 to 18 inches. Runs, tail outs and pools are 2 to 4 feet. This water changes character from gravel to baseball and softball sized rock to boulder and ledge and then back again. The banks alternate from wood-land to high bluffs and then back again. The high water conditions create a heavy froth through and below each rapid. The sound of fast water tumbling over rocks and gravel is mesmerizing. What a wonderful place.

I am intoxicated by visual beauty and the sounds of a fast flowing creek during its spring unleashing. It does not matter if this living entity is barren of steelhead. I am already having fun.

Cast and drift. Cast and drift. Cover my temples with the inside of my palms to block out excess sunlight, while visually scouring each and every possible area for movement, color change, shape, unnatural riffling of surface water or anything which could give away the presence of something good.

I recently purchased a pair of optically correct polarized sunglasses. They perform great – well worth the investment. My ability to see and make out shapes below the surface was very good. I recall a past trip to this area with a friend who had on a pair of non polarized sun glasses. I located fish for him because he could not make them out. When he borrowed my spare pair he immediately started spotting them. They often appear as a large grayish blotch on the stream bottom. A serious fisherman must have polarized sunglasses, I thought to myself while working the water. Many recommend gray lenses for bright sunny conditions while amber or brown are best for low light. I prefer amber or brown for all fishing conditions because they show clarity and shape below the surface much better than gray.

After working the water for over 2 miles I found them, a pod of unusually large steelhead. I estimated they ranged in weight from 12 to 20 plus pounds. The high water had done its job. This was the mother lode. They would probably quickly spawn and be gone in a day or two. The females were bright like a shiny dime while the males had a light reddish pink color to their sides and gill plates. They were fresh in from the lake.

It was now 4 p.m. There is nothing I can say to exactly describe the next 3 hours. You would have had to been there at my side to feel the excitement. I will try to describe the experience for you as close as possible.

In 20 years of pursuing steelhead this was the first time I found so many large fish in one place. I hardly noticed that the showers had increased to a heavy rain. Then a torrential downpour accompanied by violent lightning and thunder. Good judgement gave in to the moment. I remained. This had been my dream for many years. I may never luck into an opportunity like this again. I thought to myself that if struck by lightning my body may not be found for a week. Perish the thought.

The creek rose quickly. She turned into a mini raging river. The water discolored but I still remained as if possessed. I kept telling myself - This is the right place and the right time. The big rainbows were holding in good spawning gravel above a long turbulent rapid. About 100 feet upstream was another high velocity rapid. I felt these fish were hot to spawn and did not want to fight their way through another piece of fast water. Yikes! That lightning was close. Man, I can feel the thunder in the pit of my stomach.

Fish on! A large hen (13 to 14 pounds) took 5 feet from me, jumped and immediately made a fifty foot, blistering run, towards the rapid above. She jumped while I was trying to follow, changed direction and quickly leaped again in front of me. Before I could react, this magnificent creature became airborne again about fifty feet downstream. She made another 50 foot run, jump and then broke off. My screaming reel quickly became silent. How could she move so fast, with such power?

I retied with 10 pound instead of 8 while trying to regain my composure and develop a plan. After 2-1/2 hours of this, I still had not landed one but lost another 5 or 6. A couple snapped the line and 3 were lost on leaps and cartwheels. These fresh fish were electric. I can not imagine any fish being more so. As far as I am concerned, there is no difference in vitality and fight between a ocean run and a lake run. One huge 20 pound plus male shook free and won his freedom after a 10 minute battle and just inches from my grasp causing me to revaluate my belief that big fish seldom jump.

The creek was now way out of shape. The water resembled dark chocolate milk. The big bows were very hard to make out as they now appeared as a faint grayish blotch surrounded by dark brown water. I decided that my only chance was to switch from a number 10 green caddis nymph to a large size 2 chartreuse pattern. The tippet was replaced with 12 pound and an additional piece of shot added. I wanted to land at least one of these beautiful creatures and felt that a heavier line plus a larger, flashier fly would be in my favor.

After casting a dozen times to a large grayish blotch I began to doubt if it was really a fish. Then it happened – a hard quick take. Instinctively, I set the hook. A 20 pound buck jumped a few feet in front of me. In that magic moment, I could make out his beautiful colored flanks and gill plates, just like they were on fire and my fly stuck firmly in the corner of his mouth. What a beast.

This fish made a move downstream. My fly reel screamed. There was no slowing him down. Quickly, I followed along the edges of the rapid and around the bend, determined to land this trophy. I rounded another bend about 100 yards downstream in hot pursuit with the reel singing. Then my heart sank. Lying across the stream was a large maple and the huge rainbow had gone under and was still taking line. He jumped and then stopped. I had a chance. Slowly and smoothly, I started pumping him with the hopes of working the big steelhead back through the downed tree. It was a long shot at best but still better than no chance at all.

I had him moving now with slow easy pumps. With only another few feet to go he had enough. His next run was fast, long and strong. My reel sang and the rod bent and bucked as this huge fish of a lifetime ran around another bend and continued moving as if there was no end to his stamina. This run seemed like it lasted an hour but in reality it was only 8 or 10 seconds. The fly ripped out and he was gone. One moment I had it all – connected to the ultimate opponent and then a few seconds later - alone and beaten.

It was now 7:15 P.M. Getting out with light was imperative. I only had 20 minutes left until dark. The footing was difficult even with Korker Wading Sandals but I also had to contend with the many bluffs and increased velocity of the current. I ran the entire way. Believe me, the extra dry clothes in my truck were a welcome sight. I drove back to the B&B for a nice hot shower and then dinner at a local Pulaski restaurant. My thoughts were full of the day's experiences.

It was now time to plan for the following morning. I just wanted to land one. This became an obsession especially after the events of the day. The heavy rain continued all night stopping around 5:30 a.m. the following morning while I was having breakfast.

I drove the 10 miles to the creek but it was to no avail. She was not fishable – Zero visibility. The prospects were that perhaps she could partially clear in a day or two but another heavy rain is predicted for tomorrow. With gratitude for the previous days fishing, I packed my equipment, checked out of the motel and prepared myself for the ride home. This was the first time I had such an intense experience (adventure) like the day before and only a 5 hour drive from my home in Vermont. I could see the fish, get them to take and yet could not land a single one. It was a wonderful, challenging encounter of which, for me, to this day, there has been no equal.

The creek possessed all the charms of a beautiful woman. She could intoxicate your senses, control your emotions, stun you with her beauty, whisper sweet nothings, leave you broken and humbled, give up nothing and have you willingly begging for more. This beautiful creek had given me opportunity along with unforgettable, treasured memories. I could not stop thinking of each and every lost battle of the previous days fishing nor did I want to. Thank You Old Friend!

## Personal Fishing Experiences and Insights

The pursuit of New Hampshire and Vermont challenging trout and smallmouth bass while using a McKenzie drift boat has been my meat and potatoes for 25 years. However, a time or two in the spring and fall you will find me pursuing lake Ontario steelhead in creeks and rivers. They are a magnificent fish ranging in size from 3 to 20 plus pounds. Their electrifying acrobatics, long runs and beautiful coloration could easily make one a fitting substitute for the pot of gold at the end of a rainbow. Steelhead in rivers are a nomadic creature, here today and gone tomorrow but will hold in pools for extended periods during the winter months.

The best option for someone wanting to get in on the action is to prepare by reading and also view DVDs on the subject. Do not forget to search the internet. Then, hire a competent guide for at least your first few times out. Many guides are willing and able to share information with you in a few days which could take years to learn. Let your guide know the type of fishing you prefer be it drift fishing with a spinning rod or noodle rod or fly fishing with a standard fly rod or a longer spey.

I would like to share with you a few experiences which occurred during a few personal fishing vacations for steelhead in upstate New York.

A large buck was spotted moving into the riffles. I lost sight of him but knew he was in a certain area hidden by the turbulent water. After numerous casts with a size 10 Green Butt Skunk, he took. There wasn't even a chance to set the hook as the big rainbow hooked himself, immediately jumped and without hesitation bolted downstream.

I tried to slow him down but it wasn't happening. This trophy had quickly rounded a bend and was not stopping. I had to run along the shallow edges of the creek to keep up. Around another bend and still my reel is screaming. I remember hearing a loud noise as I was running after him and wondering what it was. This was after a quarter mile or so. It was my heavy breathing from the chase. Adrenaline was so high that I wasn't tired at all. It seemed that this loud breathing and gasping for breath was from someone else. It was my interpretation of an out of body experience which enabled me to tap into a reservoir of strength and endurance.

I ended up chasing this trout for almost a half mile. He was pulling out line so fast that on a couple of occasions the reel handle banged my knuckles, bruising and cutting them. Finally, while still running and gasping for breath the big Rainbow rolled, a sure sign he was getting tired. There was a gravel bar 60 feet downstream to the right. If I could jump this log 20 feet downstream and pressure him towards the gravel bar he would run out of water and be beached. It is only 10 feet to the log.

Oh no! My jump barely cleared the log but the spiked sandals I was wearing dragged across just enough to grab. What else can go wrong? I flew through the air and tumbled head first into 18 inch deep, 38 degree water. What a rush! I pushed myself up with my left hand while still holding onto the fly rod with my right. I was drenched. My right arm started bucking up and down. This quickly brought me back to the moment. I still had him on and still had a chance. I rose to resume the chase.

The beaching opportunity was lost because he was able to move downstream through the slot created by the gravel bar. Luck was with me. I was able to gain on him by running across the gravel bar.

He was now directly across stream from me holding in an undercut bank. I knew this wonderful creature was moments from being landed. He was exhausted. While gently applying steady pressure, I soon expected this beautiful creature to slowly give ground —but instead my line snapped. Unbelievable. Man, what more could I do? I was using an 8 pound tippet but it must have been weakened during the chase. The steelhead was still in the undercut and very tired. I couldn't see him but he had to be there.

I just could not stand it. Immediately throwing rod and reel on the bank, I dove under. I had him in my arms for a few seconds for a momentary victory but he slithered out. There was still snow on the ground and the time of year was late March. I once again struggled to my feet gasping for breath from such cold water. There he was, lazily swimming a few feet from me getting his bearings and headed downstream in 10 to 12 inches of water. My orange fly with a silver pheasant crest tail was stuck in the corner of his mouth. What a fish.

There is just something about a 20 plus pound male steelhead. One minute I was wealthy beyond belief locked in struggle with an awesome opponent and the next a second best humbling finish. A roaring rapid seemed to sing praise to two warriors for a battle well fought. A 2 plus mile soaking wet walk back to my truck was my reward along with a most regarded memory. It was more than an even trade. I would have been able to land that big beautiful steelhead if only my reel had a stronger and smoother drag. The big fish blew through the drag resistance. This is a different type of fishing than I am used to. I kept thinking that just maybe my lovely wife will surprise me by purchasing a high quality fly reel for my upcoming birthday. It is never too early to start hinting. I must have a better reel if pursuing steelhead is in my future. I had another thought while continuing the long walk back to the truck and dry clothes. What a lousy jump attempt over that log – a lucky steelhead.

There was another large steelhead opportunity blown two years ago. I had been fishing for three days in late March with a friend. The fishing was slow and the weather miserable, somewhere in the mid to upper teens each morning and warming to the low to midtwenties with constant heavy winds and snow flurries.

We fished hard for two strikes with none landed. The last day we started fishing at daybreak for 5 hours without a bite. My friend was ready to go home but was convinced to wait in the truck with the heater on while I checked out one more area.

He should have gotten out and fished. I had five fish on in an hour landing two fresh hens around 10 pounds each. These fish were all electric each breaking up the river with several jumps.

A twenty pound plus male still haunts my memory. (It's usually easy to differentiate males from the females with the colored up flanks and gill plates. The fresh females are bright silver with little coloration and a rounder shaped nose). He took on the swing with the shot placed 3 feet above the fly. I knew he was a big fish instantly.

Right away he jumped and made a move upstream. Luck was with me because as long as the big bow continued committing upstream he was also fighting the current. I lightened the pressure because it has been my experience that if too much pressure is applied on a fish that is headed up it will turn and bolt downstream. Most of the snags were downstream. Hopefully, I would be able to slowly wear him down before realizing he was hooked.

Everything worked as planned. It was 10 minutes of steady pressure before the big worn out steelhead realized trouble was brewing and made a move downstream. I regained control and tightened down on the drag to land him. This was my mistake. Just inches from landing the great fish he panicked and found the energy to muster one final, hard gallant run along with a vicious head shake. I tried to quickly loosen the drag but was too late. I had made an error in judgment, (opened a window) and the giant buck had taken advantage, made it to a sunken tree and broke me off, winning his freedom.

I would have released him anyway but to land a fish

well over twenty pounds would have been a great personal achievement. What a costly mistake - A little more patience and this trophy would have provided an enormous amount of satisfaction. I should have known better. Big fish need to be played with caution especially near the end of the fight. They always seem to find the energy for that one last powerful surge. It was a hard learned lesson and one to remember for a lifetime especially when playing a trophy in the future.

Finally, my friend arrived on the scene to see what was taking so long. He showed his class by being very gracious and congratulated me. All I could do was mumble about the one that got away.

Just last year I hooked up with a large steelhead on another beautiful creek in upstate New York. He decided it was time to take me for a long brisk walk. After a quarter mile, the big rainbow was tired but still far from landed. Just below us there was a 25 yard long shallow rapid. Slowly, but deliberately, I began to pressure him towards a beach above the rapid.

He was flopping on the edge of the current when the line snapped. Six pound line sometimes does not cut it but it is better to hook up often than to miss out on opportunities because my line is too heavy. Still, I should have used 8. I threw my rod up on the bank and ran after the steelhead yelling "Oh no, not again".

He made a couple of flops while managing to get back into the current and was drifting downstream just below my position. The big buck was in the process of righting himself which prompted my decision. I belly flopped on top of the steelhead in the foot deep rapid immediately wrapping my arms around the beautiful creature. I tumbled through the rapids with my prize held tightly while trying to kick myself to shore out of the grasp of the water's velocity. This steelhead did not get away. He was a gorgeous 18 pound, prime steelhead with a beautiful double reddish orange stripe down his side and lovely bright pink gill plates. His sperm bags were fully intact (fresh fish). I regretted killing him. The big buck gave a spectacular account of himself causing me to feel that the memory would have been enhanced if released.

While working my way out of the creek with the trophy buck, I saw another male steelhead lying above a riffle in good spawning gravel about 18 inches deep. He was about 10 pounds. I quietly got into position above then began casting a green size 10 caddis larva imitation. My fly was allowed to continue past the steelheads tail and into the rapid below before picking up for the next cast. I did not want to spook him.

Inching upstream would enable a drift to him from a slightly different angle. Lets try it. My fly drifted past the buck's nose again with zero interest. All of a sudden my heart nearly jumped through my chest. My rod was almost yanked from my hand and the reel started screaming. A bright 15 pound hen jumped three feet in the air with my fly showing in the corner of its mouth. It was a perfect moment which will last forever in memory. I wonder what the hen had thought as the fly kept drifting by her position in the rapid. I guess she finally couldn't stand it. I landed her about 100 yards downstream. Some days you got it – some days you don't. It is hard to beat dumb luck. What a great feeling it is to walk out of a creek with an 18 pound buck and the memory of a freshly released 15 pound mint bright female.

When I first arrived two gentlemen passed me on the way out of the creek. They both shared disenchantment for the area because of lack of fish. If they had only walked a little further while working good structure and carefully viewing the bottom with polarized sun glasses they wouldn't have been disappointed.

I have had over the years the chance to go on numerous fishing vacations (adventures) – Some in other countries and some many miles away from home in this country. My preference after several personal fishing experiences is spending my vacation time pursuing steelhead and salmon in upstate New York. It offers everything I desire and is less than 6 hours from my home in Vermont. (Smallmouth bass would also be at the top of my list for pursued species if I did not guide for them.).

I shared with you only a few of my memorable outings. I would like to think much was learned from each of them. I have been fortunate to land a lot of good fish and also lose a lot. In most cases the fish lost were due to:

1. Lack of proper execution
2. An error in judgment
3. Lack of patience
4. Equipment failure

Occasionally, a fish may just come off or break off but most big fish lost after being hooked will be because of one or a combination of the 4 reasons listed above.

What should be realized is that big is relative to the water fished and the equipment used. In a small brook on ultra light tackle a 12 inch brook trout is large. On most trout streams or rivers any trout over 18 inches is considered a big fish. For smallmouth bass a 4 pound specimen or larger is a trophy with largemouth bass 7 pounds or larger. Cut these numbers in half for smaller ponds or streams. A steelhead 15 pounds or larger is a trophy to me and a trophy king salmon in the northeast will weigh 35 pounds or larger.

In the movie, "A River Runs Through It" it is said there are three periods of growth and or development a fisherman or woman may go through. Not everyone makes it through the first stage and even fewer make it through the second.

The first is a desire to catch lots of fish. The second period of growths objective is to hook up often but the need to deceive, play and land a trophy is now the main focus. Each and every fish hooked causes a momentary escalation in adrenaline levels as you perceive it may be that sought after trophy.

Because of a limited resource, many folks in this day and age will carefully release a trophy caught fish in a way which ensures their survival. A picture may be taken if it does not hinder this. These folks feel a trophy fish is too valuable a resource to be caught only once. The entire game to them involves enjoyment of the ever changing never ending challenge. The more difficult the achieved goal, the greater the personal satisfaction.

The 3rd stage is usually attained only by a few. For this stage maximum enjoyment and a fulfilled appreciation is enjoyed when placing oneself in a beautiful and productive fishing environment without it necessary to fish.

My greatest satisfaction as a New Hampshire and Vermont fishing guide is making it possible for folks to enjoy themselves in a way which would be difficult on their own. However, I still enjoy deceiving, playing, landing and carefully releasing salmon, trout and smallmouth bass, especially larger ones while fly fishing or light spinning. My guess is I am somewhere between the second and third stage of development, which is a terrific place for a fishing guide to be.

It has been my experience that big fish opportunities do not present themselves every day. Once any serious angler locates one a little time should be taken to analyze the situation. Work out a plan enabling you to hook, play and land the fish taking into account everything that could possible go wrong and what to do in case it does. Remember to maintain your composure, do everything right and above all do not take a stab with your net on a green fish.

The difference between a very successful fishing person and one not so successful is knowledge, experience, observation and concentration with the ability to blend it all together while adjusting to each individual and unique situation encountered.

# Fond Memories

One thing you can count on is that everything will not be perfect every time out. You may experience that special time or times a strike occurs on almost every cast. Then there are days when you could not buy a strike. That's fishing. It is those special fishing trips which keep us hooked and coming back for a lifetime.

It is in those few special moments an everlasting memory may be created. It is not just the fish catching which makes an unforgettable memory but also the companionship which it is shared with along with scenery, weather and wildlife. This all adds up to capturing a moment. I believe a fond memory is one of the most precious things we can own, fishing related or not. All else comes and goes but a pleasant memory remains always. That moment in which we are ready to meet our maker thoughts will not drift to the possessions we accumulated throughout the years nor of the financial success we achieved. Chances are at this moment we will dwell upon our fond memories.

Let us live our lives focused towards the pursuit of as many of these as is possible to squeeze into our existence while gathering bonding experiences for ourselves and everyone we love. When we create positive situations and place ourselves in the correct places with the right frame of mind pleasurable memorable moments will occur for ourselves, family and friends.

It may be the bear that swam across the river in front of you with just its head showing, shook like a dog from head to toe after exiting and then lumbered up a steep bank, or a red tailed hawk passes overhead and screams just like in the movies. An unlucky flock of merganser ducks in flight land near the river shore beneath a huge maple containing two nesting eagles.

Further downstream you notice the melody of song birds seems always present. Were these sounds always there and you didn't notice them before? This is a concert heard long after the float is completed. A mother fox with her two frolicking pups in mid May have many months of the good life ahead before winter. A baby moose looks so friendly standing in the river ahead until a frothing, protective mother runs frantically from the shoreline woods to place itself between its baby and us, just a few feet away.

A walk down a secluded forest path during a windless snow fall seems magical. The canoe trip last year down a beautiful river surrounded by mountains, huge coniferous trees and with great companions developed bonds sure to last a lifetime. Twenty years have passed since picnicking on the grass under a huge maple with an adored friend who is now your lovely wife yet it seems so recent. While at your sons 40th birthday party tonight thoughts returned to that incredible fishing trip with a 13 year old boy in northern New Hampshire. The fish kept striking both your flies during a river float trip on a beautiful day in a magnificent setting. That was a long time ago yet seems so clean, fresh and perfect. The images still remain visually pleasant and vividly imbedded in memory. These are just a few of those special moments that remain with us always.

I remember the time surface feeding fish rose throughout the placid rivers water as our day slowly blended into dusk. High on the bank we noticed the curious eyes of a herd of dairy cows follow as our drift boat casually floats by. Interesting. Every magnificent female creature resembled a statue focused on us with only their eyes moving. This sight made it hard to concentrate on hooking that last fish or two before coming to the end of the trip a scant quarter mile away.

During a windless evening it becomes increasingly difficult to differentiate reality from reflection as our boat slowly drifts along. The dimming sunlight seems to shine its brightest the last minute or two of the day as it spreads throughout the clouds, mountains and trees, simultaneous and vividly reproducing upon the rivers glasslike surface. Priceless. It is moments like these which help us realize that true beauty can never really be duplicated by written words, picture or paint. They must be experienced in person so that the dimensional sight, sounds and essence of the moment might be consumed.

Pleasant experience opportunities which we can place into our memory banks are many. Just put yourself in a lovely outdoor setting. Fishing need not be part of the equation. I can think of nothing more healthy and refreshing than to take a step back from the hustle and bustle of the repeatable day in and day out routines we have created for ourselves.

Trout and smallmouth bass have provided entertainment and relaxation for so many beyond the fishing aspect. Some folks could be on a quest for that transitional meditative state which overwhelms an enthusiast without warning when enjoying an outdoor pursuit. It may be explained as a necessary rejuvenation to complete ourselves while once again granting clear and concise perspective as it relates individually to each person and their lives.

Most frequent beautiful outdoor places for their scenic qualities or just to relax, read a book, picnic, take pictures or enjoy the company of a friend or loved one. It is the ideal type of place to renew an old acquaintance or start a new one. Trout and smallmouth are found in many of these wonderful places. You will find other forms of satisfaction are available in their pursuit beyond a few strikes from a fish.

# About the Author:

John Marshall has offered guided fishing trips and scenic float trips on the Connecticut River from central Vermont to the Canadian border for over 25 years. He is also an expert fly caster and skilled steelhead fisherman. Not simply an expert in his field, John is also a passionate teacher who loves to pass on his skills and knowledge. A day on the water with John has made better anglers of beginners and experienced fisherman alike. A pioneer in the use of western-style Mckenzie Drift Boat fishing in eastern waters, John was one of the first and still one of the few to use a drift boat to float the Connecticut River.

His guiding service, **River Excitement,** has been featured in **Outdoor Life**, **Eastern Outdoors**, **Vermont Life,** and on Vermont Public Television's **Outdoor Journal**. You'll also find a chapter involving John in Walter Wetherell's **North of Now.**

A Culinary Institute graduate in his early years, John is known for his spectacular shoreside lunches and dinners. He's equally well known for his desire to give back to the communities and the sport he loves by donating his time, teaching skills, and float trips to organizations such as Trout Unlimited, the Outdoor Women Program, numerous trout stocking and stream cleanup projects, and many other worthy causes and public service projects.

7029529R0

Made in the USA
Charleston, SC
12 January 2011